W0252532

Unterrichtsmodell

Series Editor: Hans Kröger

Dead Poets Society

by Engelbert Thaler

Thorsten Ramme
Sep 2003

Best.-Nr. 041255 X

Schöningh

EINFACH ENGLISCH

- Arbeitsfrage
- filmische Präsentation
- Einzelarbeit
- Partnerarbeit
- Gruppenarbeit
- Unterrichts-gespräch
- Schreibauftrag
- Hausaufgabe
- Projektorientierung, offenes Unterrichtsangebot
- Aufgaben mit kreativem Ansatz
- Szenisches Spiel, Rollenspiel

Vorwort

Der Titel der Reihe **EinFach Englisch** ist Ziel und Programm zugleich. Einerseits sollen Schülerinnen und Schülern literarische Zusammenhänge erklärt und ihnen damit der Zugang zu klassischen, aber auch neueren literarischen Werken erleichtert werden, und dies soll auf sprachlich einfache Art und Weise erfolgen, wodurch man der heutigen Schülergeneration sicherlich eher gerecht werden kann als mit schwierigen und komplexen Ansätzen. Andererseits sollen Lehrkräften erprobte und aus der Praxis stammende Unterrichtsmodelle angeboten werden, die ihnen einen raschen Zugriff auf unterschiedliche Materialien ermöglichen und einen Leitfaden für die Behandlung fiktionaler Texte oder die Analyse von Filmen im Unterricht bieten. Die Modelle können direkt und ohne Umschweife eingesetzt werden, langes Einlesen und eine zeitintensive Beschäftigung mit dem Stoff sind nicht erforderlich, wodurch die Arbeit, insbesondere die Unterrichtsvorbereitung von Lehrerinnen und Lehrern, erheblich erleichtert werden kann.
Schnell erhält man einen Überblick über **Figurenkonstellation** und **Inhalt** und kann sich problemlos entscheiden, ob ein Werk für eine bestimmte Reihe geeignet ist. Man weiß vorab, welche **Klausur** mit welchen Schwerpunkten geschrieben werden kann, und kann dieses bei der konkreten Planung eines Kursabschnittes entsprechend berücksichtigen. **Arbeitsblätter** sind als Kopiervorlagen gestaltet und **Tafelbilder** sind eingebettet in die **Leitfragen** zum eigentlichen Unterrichtsgeschehen, d. h., Material, das eingesetzt werden soll, befindet sich dort, wo es gebraucht wird; langes Suchen entfällt. **Piktogramme** geben optische Hilfen und Hinweise, sodass leicht zu erkennen ist, welche **Sozial-** bzw. **Arbeitsformen** sich bei den jeweiligen Aufgaben anbieten.
Die Unterrichtsmodelle basieren auf bewährten Verfahren der Textinterpretation und der Filmanalyse, dabei fließen neuere Erkenntnisse und Ansätze zu einer modernen Textrezeption angemessen ein. Der Umfang des Materials ist auf die tatsächlichen Gegebenheiten der Unterrichtspraxis abgestimmt und es sollte möglich sein, das Unterrichtsmodell vollständig und nicht nur in Auszügen im Rahmen einer Unterrichtsreihe einzusetzen. Das Prinzip der **„Components“** ermöglicht es darüber hinaus den Benutzern, unterschiedliche Reihen zu konzipieren, die an unterschiedlichen thematischen Schwerpunkten oder methodischen Fertigkeiten orientiert sind und ganz den individuellen oder kursspezifischen Bedürfnissen angepasst werden können. Dabei erheben die Unterrichtsmodelle nicht den Anspruch der Vollständigkeit, sondern eher den der Machbarkeit und Praxisnähe.

Sprachliche Betreuung: Susan Ashworth-Fiedler
Fotos S. 3, 39, 40, 41, 47: © Cinetext, Frankfurt; **S. 42:** © defd

Website
www.schoeningh.de

E-Mail
info@schoeningh.de

im Westermann Schulbuchverlag GmbH
Jühenplatz 1–3, D-33098 Paderborn

Druck: WB-Druck, Rieden am Forggensee

Druck 5 4 3 2 1 Jahr 07 06 05 04 03

ISBN 3-14-041255-X

Alle deutschsprachigen Teile dieses Werkes folgen der reformierten Rechtschreibung und Zeichensetzung.

Components

Dead Poets Society

Component 1
Setting & Protagonists (Intensive Viewing)

1.1	Setting	viewing/listening/speaking
1.2	Cinematography	viewing/cinematographic devices/ worksheet 1
1.3	Keating's Pritchard Poetry Lesson	viewing/philosophy
1.4	First Cave Meeting	viewing/group work/poetry

Component 2
Dead & Living Poets (Workshop)

2.1	Dead Poets Come Alive	reading/evaluating/poetry/ worksheets 2-6
2.2	Classroom Cave	writing/enjoying/discussion

Component 3
Keating's Followers & Antagonists (Extensive Viewing)

3.1	Movie Time	guided viewing/worksheets 7-11
3.2	Jigsaw Time	discussion/group work/jigsaw approach

Component 4
Climax & Finale

4.1	Neil's Suicide	viewing/symbolism/ atmosphere/worksheet 12
4.2	Oh Captain, my Captain!	viewing/evaluation

Component 5
After & Beyond

5.1	Freiarbeit	material guided work/Kopiervorlagen 1-12
5.2	Presentations	presenting/discussion/evaluation

Contents

Der Film

Der Film *Dead Poets Society* (*Der Club der toten Dichter*) wurde 1989 von dem australischen Regisseur Peter Weir (*Picnic at Hanging Rock*) mit Robin Williams in der Hauptrolle gedreht. Er ist inzwischen längst zu einem Kultfilm unter den Jugendlichen avanciert. Vom Filmgenre her handelt es sich um ein *teenpic*, das die Sehnsüchte und Probleme von Jugendlichen thematisiert.
Schauplatz der Handlung ist die private Internatsschule *Welton Academy* in den Bergen Vermonts. Betuchte Amerikaner schicken ihre Sprösslinge hierher, um sie für ein Studium an einer Eliteuniversität vorzubereiten (*prep school*). Die vier Säulen dieser prestigeträchtigen Schule lauten *tradition*, *honor*, *discipline*, *excellence*. Zu Beginn des Schuljahres 1959 kommt ein neuer Englischlehrer, Mr Keating (Robin Williams), früher selbst erfolgreicher Absolvent von *Welton Academy*, an die Schule. Im Gegensatz zu seinen konventionell unterrichtenden Kollegen lehnt er Gehorsam, Unterwerfung und Auswendiglernen ab. Demgegenüber appelliert er an seine 16- bis 17-jährigen Schüler, selbstständig zu denken und zu handeln, mutig zu sein, sich zu entwickeln, den Tag zu nutzen (*Carpe Diem*) und aus ihrem Leben etwas Besonderes zu machen (*make your lives extraordinary*). Seine Werte sind *love*, *beauty*, *truth*, *justice*. Als seine Schüler aus einem alten Jahrbuch erfahren, dass er früher Mitglied im *Club der toten Dichter* war, beschließen sie, einen ähnlichen Club ins Leben zu rufen. In einer versteckten Höhle im Wald werden nachts geheime Treffen veranstaltet, bei denen im Kerzenschein Gedichte, Texte und Zitate vorgetragen werden. Die Jugendlichen, die Keating zunächst mit einer Mischung aus Verwunderung und Amüsement betrachten, geraten zusehends in den Bann des charismatischen Pädagogen. Todd Anderson überwindet unter Keatings Einfluss seine Minderwertigkeitskomplexe, kann endlich offen über seine Gefühle sprechen und tritt damit aus dem Schatten seines übermächtigen Bruders. Knox Overstreet bringt den Mut auf, einem Mädchen aus einer Nachbarschule seine Liebe zu gestehen und um sie zu kämpfen. Charlie Dalton nimmt eine neue Identität an und fordert die Zulassung von Mädchen an der Schule, womit er das ganze System herausfordert. Neil Perry ignoriert das Verbot des autoritären Vaters, Theater zu spielen. Bei einer Schulaufführung gestaltet er die Rolle des Puck in Shakespeares *A Midsummer Night's Dream* mit großartigem Erfolg. Der überstrenge Vater will ihn daraufhin in eine Kadettenanstalt schicken, was Neil zum Selbstmord treibt: Er erschießt sich mit dem Revolver seines Vaters. Bei der Suche nach einem Sündenbock für diesen Skandal gelangt man sofort zu Keating, der schließlich von der Schule verwiesen wird. Der traditionsverhaftete Direktor übernimmt persönlich die Führung von Keatings Klasse, greift zur verstaubten Poetik und vermisst die Verse mit geometrischer Präzision. In einer bewegenden Schlussszene ignorieren die Schüler die Anweisungen des tobenden Mr Nolan, steigen auf ihre Tische, skandieren *Oh Captain, my Captain* und beweisen damit, dass sie Keatings Lektion verstanden haben, die Welt stets aus einer anderen und eigenen Perspektive zu betrachten.

Die Personen

John Keating Genialer Englischlehrer oder narzisstischer Romantiker, charismatischer Pädagoge oder skrupelloser Demagoge: John Keating ist die zentrale Figur des Films. Mit unkonventionellen Unterrichtsmethoden und ideeller Unterstützung der *Dead Poets Society* bewirkt er tief greifende Veränderungen im Leben seiner Zöglinge. Im Falle Neil Perrys wird er als Alleinschuldiger für dessen Suizid verurteilt und von der Schule verwiesen. Trotzdem genießt er einen finalen Triumph, wenn die Schüler in der Abschiedsszene ihren *point of view* vertikal verändern – als symbolische Geste der Verbundenheit und persönlichen Entwicklung.

Mr Nolan Mr Nolan herrscht als gestrenger Direktor über das altehrwürdige Internat. Zusammen mit dem kleinbürgerlichen Vater von Neil personifiziert er die konservativ-autoritäre Gegenwelt zu Keatings jugendlich-individualistischem Lebensentwurf. Er setzt seine Schutzbefohlenen unter Leistungsdruck, reagiert auf Ordnungswidrigkeiten mit physischen Sanktionen und findet in seinem Antagonisten einen willkommenen Sündenbock. Die Akzeptanz der Schüler bleibt ihm freilich verwehrt.

Neil Perry Neil verkörpert den schwärmerischen Künstler, der den individualitätshemmenden Restriktionen schulischen Lebens mit außerunterrichtlichen Aktivitäten entkommen will. Schauspielerisch will er in der Rolle Pucks in Shakespeares *A Midsummer Night's Dream* debütieren, sein Vater verbietet es, Neil widersetzt sich, Mr Perry verbannt ihn in eine Militärakademie, Neil sieht als einzigen Ausweg nur die Selbsttötung.

Todd Anderson Todd leidet am Geschwistersyndrom: Dem omnipräsenten Vorbild seines großen Bruders soll er, kann er aber nicht folgen. Er reagiert mit introvertierter Ängstlichkeit. Als sein Gedicht von den Mitschülern begeistert aufgenommen wird, werden seine Blockaden aufgelöst.

Knox Overstreet Knox mimt den jugendlichen Liebhaber, der viele Hindernisse aus dem Weg zu räumen hat, bevor er von seiner Angebeteten schließlich erhört wird. Permanent zwischen Euphorie und Depression schwankend, muss er einen Nebenbuhler aus dem Feld schlagen, Alkoholexzesse überstehen, flammende Liebesschwüre zunächst ersinnen und der geliebten Chris danach coram publico präsentieren.

Charlie Dalton Charlie aka Nuwanda verwendet Gedichte als Mittel zum Zweck – *to make girls swoon*. Er wechselt seine Identität und plädiert für die Aufnahme von Mädchen in Welton. Trotz physischen und psychischen Drucks bleibt er Keating loyal bis zum Ende.

Actors

Robin Williams (Keating) Born in 1952, Robin Williams began his career as a stand-up comedian. His first big break came when he was cast as the alien in *Mork and Mindy.* Since then Williams has proved to be one of the greatest actors in such memorable films as *The World According to Garp, Good Morning Vietnam*, *Awakenings, The Fisher King*, *Aladdin*, *Mrs Doubtfire,* and his Oscar winning role in *Good Will Hunting* (1997). His favourite author is E.E. Cummings.

Norman Lloyd (Nolan) Norman Lloyd was born in 1914 and is perhaps best known for his role in the TV series *St Elsewhere*. Since *DPS* he has acted in *The Age of Innocence,* a TV remake of *The Adventures of Rocky and Bullwinkle*. He has also appeared in numerous TV series including *Star Trek: The Next Generation, Wings*, and *Seven Days.*

R. S. Leonard (Neil) Robert Sean Leonard was born in 1969 and started his acting career at Joseph Papp's New York Shakespeare Festival. His first starring role was in the classic *My Best Friend is a Vampire.* Since *DPS* he has had minor roles in *Mr and Mrs Bridge* and *The Age of Innocence* as well as more substantial ones in *Swing Kids, Killer: A Journal of Murder, The Last Days of Disco* and *Tape*. His favourite author is Rupert Brooke.

Ethan Hawke (Todd) Born in Austin/Texas in 1970, Ethan Hawke grew up in New England before moving to Princeton/New Jersey where he studied acting. His first role came in Joe Dante's *Explorers* (1985) where he co-starred with River Phoenix. Since *DPS*, his second film, he has starred in more than 30 films including *Reality Bites*, *Before Sunrise*, *Hamlet, Gattaca* and *Walking Life*. He has also published two novels and produced the music video for Lisa Loeb's *Stay*. With his wife, actress Uma Thurman, he has two children. His favourite author is Gregory Corso.

Josh Charles (Knox) Josh Charles was born in 1971. After *DPS* he starred in the TV film *Murder in Mississippi,* then in *Don't Tell Mom the Babysitter's Dead*, *Threesome* and the HBO film *Norma Jean and Marilyn*. He could also be seen in the TV series *Sports Night.*

Gale Hansen (Charlie) Born in 1961, Gale Hansen has starred in a few minor films, including *The Finest Hour* with Rob Lowe. He was also seen in the short-lived TV series *Class of '96.*

Szenenübersicht der DVD *(Chapter Survey)*

No.	***Summary***	***Time***
1	A new semester at Welton Academy begins. Inside the chapel, Headmaster Nolan delivers his speech and introduces Mr Keating. In Neil's room the boys get to know each other, and Neil faces an argument with his father about his extra-curricular activities.	0:00:00
2	Keating gives his first English lesson, in which he points out the importance of *Carpe Diem*. Knox falls in love with Chris at the Danburrys.	0:09:03
3	In the *Pritchard Poetry Lesson* Keating emphasizes his view of life. Keating and McAllister discuss realism vs romanticism. The boys first learn about *DPS*.	0:20:00
4	After some preparations the first *DPS* meeting takes place in a cave at night. Neil, Cameron, Pitts, Charlie and Meeks recite poems and tell stories.	0:30:09
5	Keating tells the students about the function of language and the necessity to change one's point of view. Neil informs Todd about his role in *A Midsummer Night's Dream*. Knox sees Chris hugging another boy. During Keating's *Soccer Lesson* the boys recite verses while kicking balls.	00:39:21
6	After getting the part of Puck, Neil fakes a letter of permission. In English class, the boys read out the poems they have written. The *Ode to Joy* scene demonstrates the boys' love of their teacher. The second cave meeting takes place.	00:49:45
7	In the *Marching Lesson* Keating asks the students to find their own walk. Todd throws away his unwanted birthday present, but is consoled by Neil. While Knox gets drunk at the Danburrys' party, the other boys have their third cave meeting. Charlie (Nuwanda) informs the others that in the school paper he has asked for girls to be admitted to Welton.	01:00:48
8	Charlie provokes Mr Nolan in the chapel and is punished in the headmaster's room. Nolan asks Keating to give up his unorthodox teaching methods. Mr Perry forbids Neil to play Puck. Knox visits Chris in her classroom and recites his love poem.	01:11:52
9	The boys watch Neil and the play at Henley Hall. After the performance Neil commits suicide in his father's study.	01:25:17
10	Nolan conducts a thorough investigation into Neil's death and identifies Keating as the scapegoat. Keating is replaced by Nolan, who gives the second *Pritchard Poetry Lesson*. Todd steps on his desk shouting "Oh Captain, my Captain."	01:43:40 02:00:06

Vorüberlegungen zum Einsatz des Films im Unterricht

Dead Poets Society kann nicht den Anspruch erheben, in die *Hall of Fame* der cineastisch herausragendsten Filme aufgenommen zu werden. Weder bricht er revolutionär mit überlieferten kinematografischen Konventionen noch mischt er Bewährtes mit Kreativem in irgendeiner innovativen Art. Er stellt ein typisches und zugleich exzellentes Beispiel des erfolgreichen Hollywood-Stils dar. Filmkritiker mögen die Nase rümpfen über Konventionalität, Oberflächlichkeit, Schwarz-Weiß-Malerei, Sentimentalität, Mystifizierung des Lehrerhelden, Ausblendung der Kategorien *race*, *gender*, *politics*. Aber die von ihnen favorisierten Filme eignen sich nur selten für das fremdsprachliche Klassenzimmer, weil sie zu anspruchsvoll für jugendliche Rezipienten sind – sprachlich, thematisch, cineastisch, diskurstheoretisch.

Aus der Sicht vieler Englischlehrerinnen und -lehrer ist der zweistündige Film, der 1989 einen Oscar für das beste Original-Drehbuch bekam, hinsichtlich mehrerer Dimensionen für den Einsatz im Unterricht zu empfehlen:
(1) sprachpraktisches Argument
Es bieten sich vielerlei Möglichkeiten, die vier Grundfertigkeiten *speaking*, *writing*, *listening*, *reading* zu üben sowie lexikalische und strukturelle Kompetenzen zu vertiefen.
(2) *film analysis*
Zu den *four basic skills* gesellt sich als fünfte Fertigkeit das *viewing comprehension*. Den Schülerinnen und Schülern können Einblicke in kinematografische Techniken gewährt werden. Sie sehen und erleben, wie Kamerablickwinkel, Landschaftsaufnahmen, Musik und Montage bestimmte atmosphärische Stimmungen evozieren, und steigern so ihre *film literacy*.
(3) *poetry*
Die Behandlung von Literatur ist ein vornehmes Richtziel in allen Lehrplänen. Der Film präsentiert herausragende Beispiele einer Gattung, die bei Schülern normalerweise alles andere als beliebt ist. Durch die stimmungsvolle Darstellung kann der Film sie dazu animieren, sich intensiver mit angloamerikanischer Poesie zu beschäftigen.
(4) Landeskunde/interkulturelles Lernen
Das Standardthema *school/education* mit seinen Bestimmungsfaktoren Unterrichtsmethoden, Lehrer, Schüler, Eltern wird hier in einem beeindruckenden Rahmen variiert. Zugleich vermittelt uns das visuell reiche Porträt der idyllisch im ländlichen New England gelegenen *prep school* Eindrücke vom Selbstverständnis der gehobenen Mittelschicht/Oberschicht im Amerika der Fünfzigerjahre.
(5) *story*
Die Handlung, die sich um ein Jahr im Leben von mehreren *high school*-Schülern und ihrem ungewöhnlichen Lehrer dreht, ist klar, emotional ergreifend und charakterzentriert, wodurch vielerlei Identifikationsangebote entstehen.
(6) Thematik
Ein Erziehungssystem, das auf Tradition, Ehre, Disziplin und Leistung basiert, wird durch die Kraft von Poesie, Spontaneität und Selbstbestimmung erschüttert. Der Film wirft viele existenzielle Fragen auf: Selbstfindung, menschliche Verantwortung, Integrität, Sexualität, *peer group pressure*, Leben und Sterben, erfülltes und verfehltes Leben, Realismus und Idealismus, Sinn des Lebens. Diese Themen sind für viele Heranwachsende von höchster subjektiver Valenz und machen diesen Film

zeitlos. Die Reizfigur Keating, von Robin Williams grandios in Szene gesetzt, fordert auch das Selbstverständnis der (männlichen) Lehrer heraus.

Als mediale Basis des Unterrichtsmodells kommt die DVD-Fassung des Films zum Einsatz (Touchstone Home Entertainment – Der Club der toten Dichter – 2002 – Nr. 100947). Die besonderen Vorzüge des Datenträgers DVD sollen dabei genutzt werden. So orientieren sich die Stundenvorschläge an den Anfangs- und Endpunkten der *menu chapters*, die per direkter Szenenanwahl – ohne langwieriges Vorspulen – angesteuert werden können. Englische *subtitles* können das Hörverständnis erleichtern, deutsche Untertitel ermöglichen *cross-lingual language teaching*. Die *extras/bonus tracks* lassen sich schließlich in der *post-viewing phase* einsetzen. Natürlich kann statt der DVD auch das VHS-Video (Touchstone Home Video – Dead Poets Society – D409472 PAL VHS) verwendet werden.

Inzwischen sind auch vielerlei Hintergrundmaterialien erhältlich. Das Buch zum Film stammt von Nancy H. Kleinbaum, die den Roman kurz nach Erscheinen der Kinofassung auf der Basis des Originaldrehbuchs schrieb (*novelization*). Eine lexikalische Arbeitshilfe bieten *Aschendorffs Vokabularien*, die auch für diesen Roman (nicht den Film) die schwierigsten Vokabeln zusammenstellen (Krapf, Hans-Georg. 1997). Eine gute Internetseite, die u.a. das gesamte Filmscript (verschiedene Versionen), Fotos und Aufgabenvorschläge bietet, ist: http://www10.pair.com/crazydv/weir/dps/
Von den Filmkritiken und Aufsätzen sind besonders zu empfehlen:

- Thal, Ortwin. 1990. „Frei sein für sich selbst. Der Club der toten Dichter." *Merz* 3, 164-168.
- Heilman, Robert. 1991. "The Great-Teacher Myth." *American Scholar* 3, 417-423 (Entmythologisierung der Keatings dieser Welt).
- Pickering, Samuel. 1991. "Speakeasy." *Virginia Quarterly Review* 4, 722-745 (das reale Vorbild – *real Keating* – für den Filmprotagonisten – *reel Keating*).

Unter den Unterrichtsmodellen lassen sich vier Stränge unterscheiden. Da sind zunächst die Vorschläge für nicht-englische Fächer wie Deutsch oder Religion (z.B. Bosold, Bernhard. 1991. „Du lebst nur einmal. – Nutze den Tag." *Materialbrief RU* 3, Deutscher Katecheten-Verein, 1-5). Dann kommen die Materialien, die sich auf das nach dem Film geschriebene Buch beziehen (z.B. Meyer, Walter. 1994/95. „Dead Poets Society – Film und Buch im Englischunterricht der Klasse 10." *Materialien der Landesmedienstelle zu Film, Funk und Schulfernsehen Englisch* 2, 27-33 – Titel irreführend, da Bezug eindeutig auf Buch). Es gibt auch Artikel, die sich speziell mit den im Buch/Film zitierten Gedichten beschäftigen (z.B. Krüger-Kahloula, Angelika. 1992. „Recycling Dead Poets: An English Unit for the Upper Grades." *Der Fremdsprachliche Unterricht* 8, 42-46.). Schließlich trifft man auf Modelle, die sich auf den Film konzentrieren; besonders hervorzuheben sind hier:

- Grindhammer, Lucille. 1993. "Hollywood in the English Language Classroom: The Dead Poets Society". *Neusprachliche Mitteilungen* 4, 244-250.
- Liebelt, Wolf (Hg.). 1994. Der Film Dead Poets Society im Englischunterricht. *Materialien zur Medienpädagogik der Landesmedienstelle Niedersachsen.*

Grindhammer segmentiert den Film in acht 15-minütige Abschnitte, die in acht 45-minütigen Unterrichtsstunden bearbeitet werden; der veranschlagte zeitliche Rahmen ist allerdings nicht einzuhalten. Zu jedem Segment stellt sie eine Vokabelliste, eine Liste von Fragen und Vorschläge für die Hausaufgabe zusammen. Liebelts Materialiensammlung ist die umfangreichste und aufschlussreichste: Er erstellt ein detailliertes Szenenprotokoll mit knapp 100 Szenen, wobei jede Szene zeitlich fixiert und mit einem Fragenkatalog (inkl. Erwartungshorizont) versehen ist. Das skizzierte Unterrichtsprojekt erstreckt sich über 30 Unterrichtsstunden. Umfangreiches Quellenmaterial (mit Vokabelliste und Abdrucken der wichtigsten Filmkritiken/Aufsätze/Unterrichtsmodelle, inkl. der o.g.) rundet das Büchlein ab.

Das hier vorgeschlagene Unterrichtsmodell geht von den folgenden didaktisch-methodischen Prämissen aus:

1. Konzentration auf den Film
Das nach dem Film geschriebene Buch zeichnet sich, wie vergleichbare Artefakte, nicht durch besondere ästhetische Qualität aus. Deshalb wird versucht, das Faszinosum des Films auszunutzen. In einer abschließenden Phase könnte aber durchaus ein Kapitel zum Vergleich herangezogen werden.

2. Methodische Variation
Methodenmonismus führt auch bei einem solch attraktiven Unterrichtsstoff wie *Dead Poets Society* bald zu Abstumpfung. Intensives Sehen zum Zwecke statarischer Analyse bestimmter Szenen ist verständnisvertiefend, aber auf Dauer ermüdend. Extensives Sehen längerer Segmente en bloc mag nicht so lerneffizient sein, entspricht aber dem natürlichen Sehprozess. Beide Sehmodi sollten geschult werden. Auch müssen zusätzlich zu Verständnisfragen weitere Lerntechniken hinzutreten.

3. *Content*-Orientierung
Communicative language teaching fordert *message before form*. Inhalt, Gehalt und Gestaltungstechniken des Films sollten im Mittelpunkt stehen, Lexis und Grammatik eine dienende Funktion erfüllen. Der weitgehende Verzicht auf systematische Wortschatzarbeit im Zusammenhang mit diesem Film erfolgt darüber hinaus aus vier Gründen. Erstens wäre sie ziemlich zeitaufwändig; zweitens gehören viele neue Vokabeln nicht zum hochfrequenten Repertoire, das die Schülerinnen und Schüler in anderen Anwendungssituationen ständig benötigen; drittens würde eine lexikalische Vorentlastung nicht erheblich zum Verstehen des Films beitragen, da die Dekodierungsprobleme eher auf Modulation, Sprechtempo und Geräuschkulisse zurückzuführen sind; viertens können zur Unterstützung der *listening comprehension* jederzeit die Untertitel eingeblendet werden. Wer dennoch auf Vokabellisten nicht verzichten möchte, kann sich bei den o.g. Modellen von Grindhammer oder Liebelt bedienen.

4. Zeitliche Beschränkung
Ein zu langes Verweilen vergällt Schülerinnen und Schülern auch die motivierendste Lerneinheit. Dieses Unterrichtsprojekt kann sich über 15 Stunden erstrecken, in abgespeckter Version (ohne Lyrikbetrachtung und *post-viewing activities*) aber auch in 8 Stunden durchgezogen werden.

5. Schwerpunktsetzung
Nicht jede Szene verdient die gleiche Intensität an Beschäftigung. Keatings erste Stunden, in denen seine Lebens- und Unterrichts-Philosophie manifest werden, sowie kinematografische Techniken in ihrer Funktionalität bedürfen besonderer Fokussierung; verschiedene andere Aspekte müssen/dürfen sich dagegen mit reduzierter Betrachtungsintensität zufrieden geben.

6. Öffnung des Unterrichts
Der Film fordert Jugendliche zu selbstständigem Denken, Perspektivenwechsel und Offenheit auf. Der darauf aufbauende Unterricht darf sich nicht auf geschlossene

Fragen konzentrieren, sondern sollte vor dem Hintergrund des hermeneutisch-rezeptionsästhetischen Ansatzes offenere Unterrichtsformen wie Stationenlernen, Freiarbeit oder Gruppenpuzzle integrieren. So kann eine Äquivalenz zwischen filmischer Aussage und unterrichtsmethodischer Form erreicht werden.

Sprachliches und thematisches Anforderungsniveau machen den Einsatz des Films ab der 10. Klasse ratsam. Die im Film aufgeworfenen Fragen sind sicher für Schülerinnen und Schüler schon ab der 9. Klasse interessant. Allerdings zeigen sich auf dieser Jahrgangsstufe lexikalische Probleme und Hörverstehensschwierigkeiten noch zu deutlich. Der Einsatz der englischen Untertitel kann das Verständnis des Films auf allen Stufen erheblich fördern.

Klausuren

Im Folgenden finden sich zwei Klausuren, die man nach der Bearbeitung des Unterrichtsmodells einsetzen kann.

Klausur 1 wurde als *viewing test* konzipiert. Als Basis dient Keatings *poem recital lesson*, eingeleitet durch eine kurze Szene, in der Todd alleine in seinem Zimmer arbeitet. Der Filmausschnitt dauert viereinhalb Minuten und befindet sich in der Mitte des sechsten Kapitels auf der DVD (51. – 55. Minute des Films). Da diese Sequenz im Unterricht lediglich kursorisch behandelt wurde (*Component 3* – extensives Sehen), kann nicht von einem zu tiefen Vorverständnis der Schülerinnen und Schüler ausgegangen werden. Vom Schwierigkeitsgrad her eignet sich die Klausur für eine 10. oder 11. Klasse. In einem ersten Schritt wird das Aufgabenblatt ausgeteilt, danach der Filmausschnitt vorgeführt, bevor schließlich die Fragen beantwortet werden.

Klausur 2 basiert auf einem argumentativen Text, der sich mit der Rolle des Protagonisten kritisch auseinander setzt. Sie ist etwas schwieriger und eignet sich für Kurse der Oberstufe.

Notizen:

Poem Recital Lesson

(DVD chapter 6, in parts)

Assignments

1. Give a short summary of the contents of this film segment. Also consider how beginning and end of the sequence are linked.
2. Analyse the cinematic means which are employed to show what Todd learns in the lesson.
3. Comment on the teaching methods and techniques used by Mr Keating in this lesson.
4. Write a short diary entry about your reactions to this English lesson. You can choose Todd's, Mr Hopkins' or Knox's point of view.

Erwartungshorizont zu Klausur 1

zu 1: Give a short summary of the contents of this film segment. Also consider how beginning and end of the sequence are linked.

- Todd tries to write a poem, does not succeed, however, and so tears the paper up in frustration.
- In English class the next day the students have to present their assignments, i.e. read out the poems they have written.
- Knox recites a love poem addressed to Chris; he looks disappointed because he feels he has not found the appropriate words to express his love; Mr Keating, however, praises this effort because Knox has dealt with a major theme both in poetry and in life: love.
- Mr Hopkins reads out a very short and simple poem; Keating rejects this poem, not because it deals with a simple theme, but because it is ordinary.
- Inspired by Mr Keating, Todd finally overcomes his inhibitions and dares to speak about his fears and nightmares in public.
- Beginning and end form a circle by focusing on the same person, i.e. Todd. But whereas at first Todd feels desperate about not being able to write a suitable poem, at the end he can be happy because he has overcome his shyness.

zu 2: Analyse the cinematic means which are employed to show what Todd learns in the lesson.

- Medium shots and close-ups of Keating emphasize his function as a role model.
- Whitman's wall picture from low angle stresses his importance: "I sound my barbaric yawp over the rooftops of the world" (blackboard).
- At the beginning when Todd is unable to speak the camera is rather static.
- With Keating's help, Todd gradually dares to speak out; the camera moves across the classroom very fast, reflecting Todd's agitated mood.

zu 3: Comment on the teaching methods and techniques used by Mr Keating in this lesson.

- Creative, student-centred assignment (writing one's own poem)
- Open teaching style
- Personal and constructive evaluation of the various poems (praising, encouraging, criticizing)
- Cynical remark towards Mr Hopkins ("Congratulations, Mr Hopkins, you have the first poem that has a negative score on the Pritchard scale.")
- Rejection of a formalistic and academic approach to poetry (anti-Pritchard)
- Ability to inspire and influence students

zu 4: Write a short diary entry about your reactions to this English lesson. You can choose Todd's, Mr Hopkins' or Knox's point of view.

- Todd: This morning I had my worst and best English lesson. We had to read out our poems, and Keating picked me, of course. First I couldn't ...But then .....
- Mr Hopkins: I'm so cool. I really am. "The cat sat on the mat." That's the poem I read out in Keating's class today. All the boys grinned. Only Keating said it was ordinary.....
- Knox: Oh Chris! I love you. Do you like this poem? I read it out in class today, and Keating thought it was fine – because it's about love – and that's a major theme in life and poetry. I'm not sure if you .....

A Film Review

Keating begins another lecture by having the students rip out an introduction by J. Evans Pritchard because he thinks it is an excrement. This demonstrates his inability to teach a realistic style which conflicted with his overall romantic outlook on life. By ignoring the contrast between realism and romanticism, his teaching was biased and aided his students in their indulgence into romanticism. From the perspective of Keating's students romanticism allowed far more freedom than realism, and once they were confronted with an option they could embrace, romanticism became the compelling choice. It was the rebel movement away from the strict rules of the school and presented a fresh outlook on life.

Keating does try to elaborate on his message. The DPS inspired the poets to become romantics who had no leader, no discipline, and no direction other than that of their passions. Keating knew where that would lead them, and once he realized his students were following a similar path, he tried in vain to warn them of the consequences. For example, when Nwanda pulls his "phone call from God" stunt, Keating makes it very clear that he doesn't approve. He says, "There is a time for daring and a time for caution, and a wise man knows which is called for." He claims, "Sucking the marrow out of life doesn't mean choking on the bone." I think he did this because although he was a romantic, he had learned that discipline and tradition were essential to maintaining a well balanced life. It was the school's strong academic tradition and discipline that moulded Keating into the scholar and teacher he was. I do think Keating tried to be the anti-romantic romanticist that he preached, but at times, his passion clouded his ability to judge the outcome. His flaw in teaching the message was that he only portrayed the good points of following one's passion and he downplayed the consequences of following one's passion to extreme until he absolutely had to.

Keating's downfall begins with Neil. He is blamed for Neil's disobedience to his father, and when Mr. Perry tells him to stay away from Neil, Keating realizes he is staring directly into the face of the madman at his window. In this movie, if one were to designate a martyr or a "Christ-like" figure (as many literary critics do), Keating would be that character.

Todd was the one student Keating managed to "save" with his message. Todd realized he did have a verse to contribute, but he did not need to contribute it by extreme measures. A simple standing on his desk was enough to show that he understood Keating. In that act, Todd becomes the leader as Knox, Pitts and Meeks followed soon after. Cameron, however, refuses to stand at the end. It is probably safe to conclude that Knox followed because this was a romantic act and another way to speak out against tradition. Meeks and Pitts, on the other hand, probably did so because Keating did inspire them (whether they

truly understood as Todd did is questionable). Regardless, this act proves that at least one person grasped the message and that Keating's symbolic death was not in vain.
I believe that was the reason Keating came back to get his things during class, and he was not disappointed in Todd and his other students. He probably did feel responsible in some way for Neil's death, that he could have warned him or tried harder to "save" him, along with the other complex plethora of emotions a suicide of someone close brings with it. Seeing that some of his students did not blame him and that they understood Keating's message was genuine probably helped to renew his faith in his teaching methods, thus leading to his rebirth.

http://www.deliriumsrealm.com/delirium/movies/dps_keating.asp

Assignments

1. Outline the structure the author gives his review in order to create a concise portrait of the protagonist of the film.
2. Explain what Keating intends to say with the following two aphorisms addressed to Charlie. Do not use the underlined words.
   2.1. "There is a time for daring and a time for caution, and a wise man knows which is called for." (lines 20/21)
   2.2. "Sucking the marrow out of life doesn't mean choking on the bone." (lines 22/23)
3. Summarize the negative points the author sees in Keating's teaching style.
4. The author calls Keating "a martyr or a 'Christ-like' figure" (line 38). Comment on this classification.

Erwartungshorizont zu Klausur 2

Zu 1: Outline the structure the author gives his review in order to create a concise portrait of the protagonist of the film.

- Chapter 1: Keating's preference for romanticism (vs realism)
- Chapter 2: Keating's attempt to be an "anti-romantic romantic"
- Chapter 3: Keating's downfall
- Chapter 4: Keating as saviour
- Chapter 5: Keating's rebirth

Zu 2: Explain what Keating intends to say with the following two aphorisms addressed to Charlie:
2.1. Sometimes you have to be courageous, at other times you have to be careful. And to become a wise man, you have to distinguish between the two.
2.2. Living life to its fullest does not include doing things which are dangerous or bad for you.

Zu 3: Summarize the negative points the author sees in Keating's teaching style.
- "biased teaching": he was not able to teach in a realistic way ⇒ seduced his students to follow romanticism (chapter 1)
- Keating's passion was stronger than his reason ⇒ ignored the long-term consequences for his students (chapter 2)

Zu 4: The author calls Keating "a martyr or a 'Christ-like' figure" (line 38). Comment on this classification.

- Martyr: person who is put to death or caused to suffer greatly for his (religious) convictions
- Keating's symbolic death, i.e. his removal from teaching
- Keating sacrificed the love of his life, i.e. teaching to give his students a taste of "living"
- Keating as victim or scapegoat of administrators and parents
- Parallels to the crucifixion story of Jesus in the Bible (Jewish scribes and Pharisees, false accusations, followers)

Notizen:

Konzeption des Unterrichtsmodells

Die auf Seite 12 genannten sechs methodisch-didaktischen Prämissen – Behandlung des Films und nicht des Buches, lernzielorientierte Abwechslung der Unterrichtsverfahren, *content before form*, Vermeidung einer zeitlich ausufernden Behandlung, Setzung nahe liegender Schwerpunkte, Aufbrechen des geschlossenen Unterrichts durch Einbindung offener Ansätze – sollen in den folgenden *Components* umgesetzt werden:

Der **erste *Component*** fokussiert das erste Drittel des Films. Im Mittelpunkt steht der Protagonist John Keating mit seiner Lebensphilosophie und seinen unkonventionellen Unterrichtsmethoden. Daneben sollen filmspezifische Gestaltungstechniken besonders beleuchtet werden. Damit die Schülerinnen und Schüler die grundlegenden Determinanten des Films wie *setting*, Personen, Thematik, Atmosphäre genau kennen lernen, ist hier intensives Sehen von kürzeren Filmsegmenten mit wiederholtem Einsatz der Pause-Taste und Verständnisfragen vonnöten.

***Component* 2** stellt einen *Stopover* dar, da die Präsentation des Films unterbrochen und eine kurze Auseinandersetzung mit Lyrik angestrebt wird. Nachdem das erste Film-Drittel mit dem *cave meeting* endete, sollen jetzt die Schülerinnen und Schüler Gelegenheit bekommen, einige der rezitierten Gedichte näher zu begutachten. Um die Distanz vieler Schülerinnen und Schüler zu diesem allgemein unpopulären Unterrichtsgenre nicht zu steigern, wird auf profunde linguistisch-strukturalistische Lyrikanalyse bewusst verzichtet. Statt ganzer Texte werden kürzere Exzerpte angeboten. Die subjektive Annäherung und Aneignung der einzelnen Schüler soll angestrebt werden.

Der **dritte *Component*** behandelt den Großteil des Films – ca. 45 Minuten vom Ende des ersten DPS-Treffens bis kurz vor der Aufführung von *A Midsummer Night's Dream*. Im Gegensatz zu *Component* 1 wird jetzt der Film en bloc gezeigt, da das wesentliche filmische Verständnis bereits gelegt wurde und eine fragmentierte Rezeption nicht dem natürlichen Sehvorgang entspricht. Um einen passiven Konsum zu vermeiden und das Grobverständnis abzusichern, werden unterschiedliche Sehaufträge an Gruppen vergeben.

***Component* 4** konzentriert sich auf Klimax und Finale des Films: erfolgreiche Aufführung der Shakespeare-Komödie mit einem herausragenden Puck, Neils Suizid, Keatings Suspendierung und der bewegende Vertrauensbeweis der Schüler für ihren geliebten Lehrer. Die subjektiven Reaktionen der Schüler auch und besonders auf emotionalem Terrain sollen hier zum Ausdruck gebracht werden.

Der **letzte *Component*** widmet sich der *post-viewing phase*. Im Rahmen von Freiarbeit werden verschiedene Aktivitäten angeboten, deren Auswahl dem Ermessen der Lehrerin/des Lehrers überlassen bleibt. Je nach Interesse und Zeitbudget kann diese Phase mehr oder weniger intensiv gestaltet werden.

Component 1: Setting & Protagonists

1.1 Setting

Das erste Segment der DVD (9 Minuten) fungiert als filmische Exposition, indem es den Schauplatz der Handlung eindrucksvoll darstellt, die Protagonisten einführt und Konflikt/Thematik andeutet. Die *credits* laufen über die Stimmungsbilder der *Welton Academy Chapel*, wo die letzten Vorbereitungen für die Eröffnungszeremonie getroffen werden. Mr Nolan, der Direktor der Institution, hält seine Eröffnungsrede und stellt den neuen Englischlehrer, Mr Keating, vor. Anschließend lernen wir die wichtigsten Schüler kennen und beobachten einen von ihnen, Neil Perry, in einer ersten Auseinandersetzung mit seinem Vater.

Als *pre-viewing activity* zum ganzen Film kann zunächst das Hintergrundwissen der Schülerinnen und Schüler aktiviert werden, indem man fragt, wer den Film schon gesehen hat. Um die Spannung nicht unnötig zu vermindern, sollten nicht zu viele Details verraten werden. Als weiterer Gesprächsimpuls eignet sich das Schlussfoto des Films (vgl. Einstiegsseite), das beschrieben und interpretiert wird.

Nach dieser kurzen Hinführung wird die neunminütige Einleitung in Intervallen betrachtet. Der DVD-*Player* wird 11-mal mit der Pause-Taste angehalten. Auf jeden *freeze frame* folgen Fragen, ergänzende Informationen des Lehrers und die sukzessive Erstellung des Tafelbildes (vgl. unten).

Freeze frame 1 (vor Nolans Rede):

What impression do we get of this school?
elite school with long tradition, rich people (cars), students with blazers

Freeze frame 2 (nach Nolans Rede):

What sort of school is Welton Academy according to its headmaster?
"the best preparatory school in the United States"

Whom does he introduce?
Mr Keating, the new English teacher

What are the "four pillars" of Welton Academy?
tradition, honor, discipline, excellence

Do you like Mr Nolan? And Mr Keating?
Nolan: strict, authoritarian, conceited – Keating: nice, confident

Freeze frame 3 (nach der Freiluft-Szene – 2x vorspielen):

How does Nolan put Todd Anderson and Neil Perry under pressure?
- to Todd: "You have some big shoes to fill, young man. Your brother was one of our finest."
- to Neil: "Neil, we expect great things from you this year!"

Freeze frames 4, 5, 6, 7, 8, 9 (zur klaren Identifizierung der Schüler):

What is the name of the student in this picture?
Neil Perry, Todd Anderson, Cameron, Steven Meeks, Charlie Dalton, Knox Overstreet

Freeze frame 10 (vor Eintritt Mr Perry):

What is the boys' four-pillar version?
travesty, horror, decadence, excrement

What is Welton's nickname?
Hell-ton

Freeze frame 11 (nach Auseinandersetzung Neil – Vater):

What is this argument about?
Mr Perry thinks that Neil has too many extra-curricular activities, forbids him to be editor of the school magazine

Do you like – or understand – Mr Perry?

strict, authoritarian, caring?

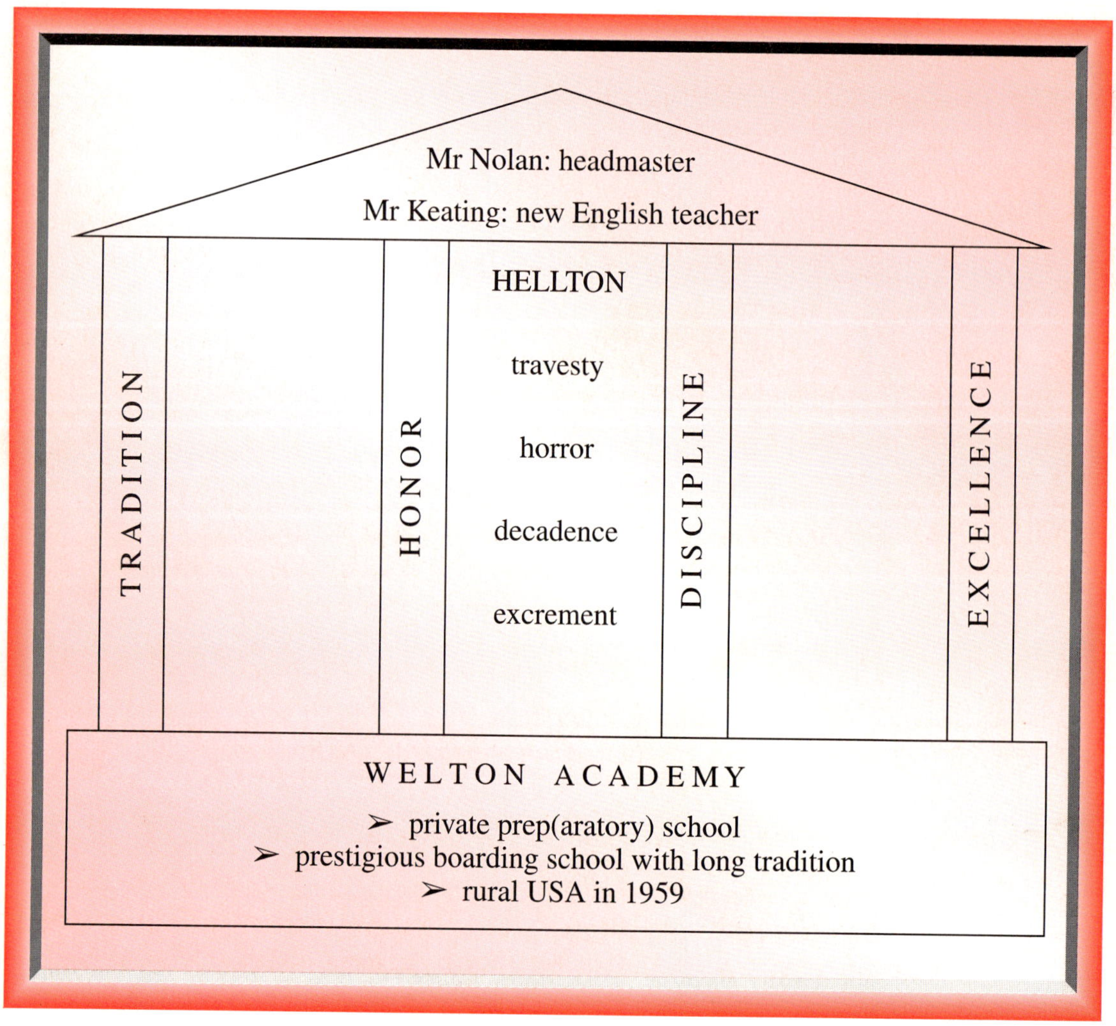

Zum Abschluss wird die Hausaufgabe gestellt:

In about 100 words, try to characterize the six boys (Neil, Todd, Cameron, Steven, Charlie, Todd) from what you have already heard and seen.

Dazu wird die Szene in Neils Zimmer ein 2. Mal vorgespielt und die Schüler machen sich Notizen, um die Aufgabe zu Hause schriftlich bearbeiten zu können.

1.2 Cinematography

Die zweite Stunde bearbeitet *Chapter* 2 (*Seize the Day*) der DVD. Dieses Segment (11 Minuten) reicht von der symbolischen Landschaft-mit-Enten-Szene bis zum Radio-Experiment im Studierzimmer und präsentiert die erste Englischstunde des unkonventionellen Lehrers.

Am Stundenanfang (nach einer möglichen Rechenschaftsablage/Wiederholung) wird die schriftliche Hausaufgabe besprochen (Charakterisierung der sechs Schüler). Folgende Merkmale könnten genannt und sollten an der Tafel fixiert werden:

- Neil: great things expected from him, seems well-liked and respected
- Todd: shy and withdrawn, afraid of having to follow in his genius brother's footsteps
- Cameron: nosy, bootlicking
- Stephen: red-haired with glasses, very good at school (Latin)
- Charlie: easy-going, smirk on his face, bad at school (flunked Latin)
- Knox: nice and good-looking

Der thematische Schwerpunkt der Stunde liegt auf kinematografischen Techniken. Zum besseren Verständnis wird ein Arbeitsblatt (*Worksheet* 1) ausgeteilt, das ein Szenenprotokoll und Fragen zu fünf spezifischen Filmtechniken enthält: Symbolismus, Sympathielenkung, Atmosphäre, Montage, *foreshadowing*. Die Szenenbeschreibungen werden vorgelesen, unbekannte Vokabeln erklärt und die Fachtermini erläutert. Danach wird das DVD-Segment ohne Unterbrechung vorgeführt. Im Anschluss diskutiert man gemeinsam die Fragen auf dem Arbeitsblatt und lässt Stichpunkte notieren.

Lösungen zu Worksheet 1:

1. parallel to boys on the staircase: noisy, wild, starting something new, breaking free
2. other teachers as *foils* to Mr Keating, to emphasize how different Keating is, to direct the viewers' sympathies to Keating
3. strange, spooky – mysterious sound, old photos, camera angle (from behind pupils' backs), Keating's position: behind pupils, whispering – to highlight Keating's unorthodox teaching style and his personality ("different, weird, spooky")

4. contrastive montage: talking, action vs silence, loneliness (Todd) – to highlight Todd's problem
5. visual (countryside) and musical (harp music) beauty/romanticism foreshadow the following love scene

Als schriftliche Hausaufgabe bietet sich eine kurze Zusammenfassung von Keatings Lebensphilosophie an:

After reflecting on Keating's first English lesson, explain his philosophy of life.

Notizen:

Cinematography

Scenes

Scene no.	*Contents*	*Time (min.sec.)*
1	Countryside with ducks	00.00
2	Boys on the staircase	00.17
3	Chemistry, Latin and trigonometry classes	00.35
4	Keating's *Carpe Diem lesson*	00.47
5	Students leaving class	06.35
6	Boys in the showers	06.59
7	Todd in his room	07.29
8	Dr Hager and Knox on their way to the Danburrys	07.56
9	Knox at the Danburrys	08.37
10	Radio experiment in the study hall	09.26 – 10.47

Film techniques

1. Symbolism
What is the function of the birds in scene 1?

2. Directing Sympathy
Why do the glimpses at chemistry, Latin and trigonometry classes precede Keating's first English lesson?

3. Atmosphere
What atmosphere is created in the Honor Room (scene 4)? How and why is this done?

4. Montage
How are scenes 6 and 7 linked?

5. Foreshadowing
How does scene 8 foreshadow the ninth scene?

1.3 Keating's *Pritchard Poetry Lesson*

Im Zentrum der 3. Stunde steht *The Pritchard Poetry Lesson*, in der Keating der trockenen, formalistischen, akademischen Herangehensweise an Lyrik, exemplifiziert an dem poetologischen Artikel eines gewissen Mr J. Evans Pritchard PhD, seinen emotional-rezeptionsästhetisch-schüleraktivierenden *approach* entgegensetzt. Die 10-minütige Sequenz beginnt im Klassenzimmer und endet auf dem Schulhof, wo die Jungen Keating über die *Dead Poets Society* ausfragen.

Zu Beginn wird die Hausaufgabe der Vorstunde besprochen, was in folgendes Tafelbild münden kann:

> Keating's philosophy of life:
> Life does not last forever (men will "fertilize daffodils") ⇒
> – "Seize the day!"
> – "Make your lives extraordinary!"
> – "Gather ye rosebuds while ye may!"

Danach wird die DVD-Sequenz ohne Unterbrechung zum 1. Mal vorgeführt und mit einfachen Fragen das Globalverständnis überprüft.

What does Keating order his pupils to do?

to rip out the introductory pages from their poetry textbook

Why does he hate Pritchard's approach to poetry?

too formalistic and academic, measures the value of a poem by statistical means

Who hesitates longest to rip out the pages and what is its effect on the viewer?

Cameron – appears as an unpleasant character

What do Keating and McAllister disagree upon?

aim of school education – make pupils have dreams or not

What is Keating telling the boys?

about the DPS

What is Neil trying to do at the end?

to reconvene the DPS

Nach diesen Globalfragen zeigt man die Sequenz ein zweites Mal. Um das Detailverstehen noch zu erleichtern, werden die englischen Untertitel eingeblendet. Im Anschluss liest die Lehrperson 10 unvollständige Sätze vor, welche die Schülerinnen und Schüler komplettieren müssen. Auf der Basis dieser Antworten und des klärenden Unterrichtsgesprächs wird das Tafelbild (vgl. S. 27) entwickelt.

1. "You will learn to ….." (think for yourselves)
2. "Words and ideas ….." (can change the world)
3. "We read and write poetry because we are members of the human race and the human race is filled ….." (with passion)
4. "The noble pursuits necessary to sustain life" are 1. ….. 2. ….. 3. ….. 4. ….. (medicine, law, business, engineering)
5. The four things "we stay alive for" are 1. ….. 2. ….. 3. ….. 4. ….. (poetry, beauty, romance, love)
6. "That the powerful play goes on and you may ….." (contribute a verse)
7. "Show me the heart unfettered by ….. (foolish dreams) and I'll show you a happy man."
8. "Only in their ….. (dreams) can men be truly free."
9. The Dead Poets "were dedicated to ….." (sucking the marrow out of life)
10. With poetry you can make women ….. (swoon)

The Pritchard Poetry Lesson

realism		***romanticism***
Medicine Law Business Engineering	⇔	Poetry Beauty Romance Love
Mr McAllister ⇓ "the heart unfettered by foolish dreams"		Mr Keating ⇓ "suck the marrow out of life"

Als Hausaufgabe können die Schülerinnen und Schüler zwischen zwei schriftlichen Aufgaben wählen:

1. Are you a realist or a romantic/an idealist? Say why.
2. "You will learn to think for yourselves." Comment on Keating's statement.

1.4 First cave meeting

Die 9-minütige DVD-Sequenz (*The Reconvening of the Dead Poets Society*) beginnt im Studierraum, wo die Jungs den Plan der Höhle (Ort der DPS-Versammlungen) studieren, und endet mit den Glockenschlägen, welche sie zur Schule zurücklaufen lassen. Im Mittelpunkt dieser Einheit steht das erste Höhlentreffen der DPS.

Die schriftliche Hausaufgabe der Vorstunde kann zur Korrektur eingesammelt oder am Stundenbeginn mündlich besprochen werden, indem pro Thema zwei Schüler ihre Ergebnisse vortragen, die anschließend verglichen und beurteilt werden.

Vor der Präsentation des neuen Filmausschnitts werden drei Gruppen gebildet, die unterschiedliche Sehaufträge erhalten. Die *pre-cave group* fokussiert die Atmosphäre vor der Versammlung, die *in-cave group* beobachtet das Geschehen während der Sitzung, die dritte Gruppe konzentriert sich auf die Rolle Neils vor und während des Treffens. Als gedankliche Stütze dient eine Tabelle (Folie oder Tafel), deren erste drei Spalten (*group*, *topic*, *task*) vor der Darbietung ausgefüllt werden, während die letzte Spalte nach dem Sehen bei der Besprechung der Gruppenergebnisse ergänzt wird.

Group	Topic	Task	Answers
1	Pre-cave atmosphere	How is the spooky atmosphere during the boys' walk to the cave created? Consider music, noises, light, clothing and images.	– eerie music – squeaking door, barking dog, howling wolf, flying birds – darkness, shadows, flashlight beams – KKK-like hoods – deserted corridor, owl, moon
2	In-cave ambience	What elements contribute to the success of the first meeting? Observe what the boys do and say.	Combination of – solemnity (Neil's opening) – mystery (Neil's ghost story) – awkwardness (Cameron's "joke") – humour (Pitts' poem) – eroticism (Charlie's pin-up girl and love poem) – inspiration (Neil's *Ulysses*) – action ("Then I saw the Congo") – cosiness (picnic) – romanticism (candlelight)
3	Neil's role	How does Neil behave in this segment? Pay attention to what he does, finds, says and intends.	– persuades Todd to join the DPS – finds DPS anthology on his desk – opens the meeting – tells a ghost story – reads Tennyson's Ulysses – instigates the second DPS

Die Ausführungen der 3. Gruppe leiten über zum zweiten Stundenabschnitt, der Neils Rezitation von Tennysons Gedicht *Ulysses* intensiver betrachtet. Je nach Zeitbudget, Interesse und Zielsetzung können folgende Optionen gewählt werden (da dieses Gedicht in längerer Fassung auch in *Component 2* bearbeitet wird, können hier Kürzungen bedenkenlos vorgenommen werden):

- Zweites Sehen/Hören von Neils Vortrag ohne Untertitel
- mündliche oder schriftliche Zusammenfassung der Grundaussage des Gedichtauszugs (appeal to discover other worlds, new horizons, one's own identity)
- erneutes Sehen/Hören mit englischen Untertiteln zur Verständniserleichterung
- Sehen mit englischer Tonspur und deutschen Untertiteln: Analyse der Übersetzung
- Sehen mit englischen Untertiteln bei abgeschaltetem Ton: Schüler rezitieren
- Herausarbeitung und Bewertung von Neils Intention (by reciting Tennyson's poem he invites the others to begin their individual quests – judgments may vary)

Als Hausaufgabe bietet sich hier eine Internet- oder Bibliotheks-Recherche zu Autor (Alfred Lord Tennyson) und Protagonist (Ulysses) des Gedichts an.

Notizen:

Component 2: Dead & Living Poets

2.1 Dead poets come alive

Nach dem intensiven Sehen des 1. Teils folgt nun ein kurzer *Stopover*, um einige Gedichte näher zu beleuchten. Dieser *poetry workshop* findet zunächst in Form von *Stationenlernen* (*Lesezirkel*) statt. Es werden fünf Stationen (vier Tische in den Ecken, einer in der Mitte des Klassenzimmers) aufgebaut, an denen jeweils ein Gedicht (Arbeitsblatt in Klarsichtfolie oder laminiert) in gekürzter Form aufliegt. Die fünf Exzerpte (vier Gedichte, ein Prosaauszug) sind:

1. Walt Whitman: *O Me! O Life!*
2. Henry David Thoreau: *Walden*
3. Alfred Lord Tennyson: *Ulysses*
4. Robert Frost: *The Road Not Taken*
5. William Shakespeare: *Sonnet 116*

An jeden Text sind die selben vier Aufgaben angehängt: Lesen der Verse – Nachschlagen unbekannter Wörter, sofern sie für das Textverständnis unbedingt vonnöten sind – Diskussion der Intention/Botschaft – persönliche Wertung. Auf jedem Tisch liegt ein zweisprachiges Wörterbuch aus, auf dessen sparsamen Gebrauch aber deutlich hingewiesen wird. Entsprechend den fünf Gedichten/Stationen werden fünf Gruppen gebildet, die sich im Uhrzeigersinn von einer Station zur nächsten begeben und ihre Aufgaben erledigen. Pro Station werden ca. sechs Minuten veranschlagt; auf die Einhaltung der Unterrichtssprache Englisch muss geachtet werden. In der verbleibenden Zeit der Unterrichtsstunde erhalten die Schülerinnen und Schüler die folgende Aufgabe, die sie in der Schule und zu Hause bis zur nächsten Stunde erledigt haben müssen:

Among your group, first decide on one of the five poems that appeals to you most. Second, prepare a recital of this poem for the next lesson – by one student, by several students alternately, or in chorus form.
Third, be prepared to state in class what the message of this poem is and why you like it.
You may also look for some accessories to make your presentation in class more vivid.

Notizen:

Walt Whitman (1819–1892)
O Me! O Life!

O me! O life!
Of the questions of these recurring,
Of the endless trains of the faithless,
Of cities fill'd with the foolish, ...
What good amid these, O me, O life?

A n s w e r

That you are here – that life exists and identity,
That the powerful play goes on, and you may contribute a verse.

Whitman, W. 1976. *Leaves of Grass, Book XX* (1881). Secaucus: Longriver, 221

Tasks:

1. Read the poem.
2. Consult the dictionary only if necessary. Do not look up every unknown word.
3. What does the poet intend to say?
4. Does this poem appeal to you? Say why (not).

Henry David Thoreau (1817–1862)
Walden

I went to the woods because I wanted to live deliberately,
to front only the essential facts of life,
and see if I could not learn what it had to teach and not,
when I came to die,
discover that I had not lived.
I did not wish to live what was not life,
living is so dear;
nor did I wish to practise resignation,
unless it was quite necessary.
I wanted to live deep and suck out all the marrow of life,
to live so sturdily and Spartan-like as to put to rout all that was not life,
to cut a broad swath and shave close,
to drive life into a corner,
and reduce it to its lowest terms.

Thoreau, H.D. 1960. *Walden* (1854). New York: Signet, 66.

Tasks:

1. Read the poem.
2. Consult the dictionary only if necessary. Do not look up every unknown word.
3. What does the poet intend to say?
4. Does this poem appeal to you? Say why (not).

Alfred Lord Tennyson (1809–1892)
Ulysses

Come my friends,
'Tis not too late to seek a newer world.
Push off, and sitting well in order smite
The surrounding furrows; for my purpose holds
To sail beyond the sunset, and the baths
Of all the western stars, until I die.
It may be that the gulfs will wash us down.
It may be that we touch the Happy Isles,
And see the great Achilles, whom we knew.
Though much is taken, much abides; and
though
We are not now that strength which in old
days
Moved earth and heaven; that which we are,
we are;
One equal temper of heroic hearts,
Made weak by time and fate, but strong in
will
To strive, to seek, to find, and not to yield.

Campbell, O.J./Pyre, J.F.A. (eds.). 1971. *English Poetry of the Nineteenth Century.* Westport: Greenwood, 397f.

Tasks:

1. Read the poem.
2. Consult the dictionary only if necessary. Do not look up every unknown word.
3. What does the poet intend to say?
4. Does this poem appeal to you? Say why (not).

Robert Frost (1875–1963)
The Road Not Taken

Two roads diverged in a yellow wood,
And sorry I could not travel both
And be one traveler, long I stood
And looked down one as far as I could
To where it bent in the undergrowth;

Then took the other, as just as fair,
And having perhaps the better claim,
Because it was grassy and wanted wear;
Though as for that the passing there
Had worn them really about the same,

And both that morning equally lay
In leaves no step had trodden black.
Oh, I kept the first for another day!
Yet knowing how way leads on to way,
I doubted if I should ever come back.

I shall be telling this with a sigh
Somewhere ages and ages hence:
Two roads diverged in a wood, and I
I took the one less traveled by,
And that has made all the difference.

Allen, G.W./Rideout, W.B./Robinson, J.K. (eds.). 1965. *American Poetry.* New York: Harper & Row, 668.

Tasks:

1. Read the poem.
2. Consult the dictionary only if necessary. Do not look up every unknown word.
3. What does the poet intend to say?
4. Does this poem appeal to you? Say why (not).

William Shakespeare (1564–1616)
Sonnet 116

Let me not to the marriage of true minds
Admit impediments. Love is not love
Which alters when it alteration finds,
Or bends with the remover to remove.
O no, it is an ever-fixed mark
That looks on tempests and is never shaken;
It is the star to every wandering bark,
Whose worth's unknown, although his height be taken.
Love's not time's fool, though rosy lips and cheeks
Within his bending sickle's compass come;
Love alters not with his brief hours and weeks,
But bears it out even to the edge of doom.
If this be error and upon me proved,
I never writ, nor no man ever loved.

Wells/Taylor (eds.). 1987. *The Complete Oxford Shakespeare.* Oxford: OUP, 390.

Tasks:

1. Read the poem.
2. Consult the dictionary only if necessary. Do not look up every unknown word.
3. What does the poet intend to say?
4. Does this poem appeal to you? Say why (not).

Erwartungshorizont zur Frage 3 (author's intention):

Walt Whitman: *O Me! O Life!*
(Worksheet 2)
- looks at the defective world
- questions the meaning of life
- affirms life despite problems
- encourages readers to make their lives extraordinary

Henry David Thoreau: *Walden*
(Worksheet 3)
- goes back to nature
- tries to find deeper meaning through isolation from society and introspection
- probes into the essential facts

Alfred Lord Tennyson: *Ulysses*
(Worksheet 4)
- Ulysses looks back on his travels, describes present and predicts future
- summons up courage in the face of death
- asks readers to discover new horizons
- warns people not to give up when confronted with obstacles

Robert Frost: *The Road Not Taken*
(Worksheet 5)
- employs a country image
- stresses the importance of making decisions
- points out the necessity of going one's own way
- accepts going this way alone

William Shakespeare: *Sonnet 116*
(Worksheet 6)
- declares the permanence of love
- emphasizes spiritual love

2.2 Classroom cave

Die Präsentation der Gruppenergebnisse der vorangehenden Stunde erfolgt – analog zu den geheimen Treffen der DPS – in dem zur Höhle umgewandelten Klassenzimmer. Dazu muss lediglich der Raum verdunkelt werden; ein Tisch wird in der Mitte platziert, auf den ein weißes Tuch gelegt wird; ein großer Kerzenständer sorgt für quasi-romantische Atmosphäre und die nötige Helligkeit zum Lesen. Die Schülerinnen und Schüler können sich auf den Boden setzen.
Die Lehrerin/der Lehrer eröffnet das Treffen, indem sie/er eine alte Lyrikanthologie (oder ähnlich Aussehendes) hochhebt und den folgenden Prolog deklamiert:

J Keating
DEAD
POETS
'42

FIVE CENTURIES OF VERSE

To Be Read At The Opening
of D. P. S. Meetings

I went to the woods because I
wanted to live deliberately ...
I wanted to live deep and suck
out all the marrow of life!
To put to rout all that was not life ...
And not, when I came to die, discover
that I had not lived ...

H.D.T

D.P.S

Nach diesem feierlichen Zeremoniell trägt jede Gruppe ihr Lieblingsgedicht vor inklusive Darlegung der Botschaft und Begründung für die Wahl.

Sollte Zeit übrig bleiben, bieten sich folgende Aktivitäten an:

- Vergleich der verschiedenen Vorträge
- Erörterung, warum andere Gedichte nicht gewählt wurden
- Darbietung eines zusätzlichen Gedichts durch die Lehrperson

Zum Ende werden als Vorbereitung für die nächste Stunde die Arbeitsblätter an fünf Gruppen ausgeteilt mit der Aufforderung, die Fragen zu studieren und unbekanntes Vokabular zu klären (vgl. *Component 3 – Worksheets* 7–11).

Notizen:

Component 3: Keating's Followers & Antagonists

3.1 Movie time

Nach dem poetischen *Stopover* wird nun der Großteil des Films gezeigt. War bei den ersten 40 Minuten intensives Sehen gefordert, so werden die nächsten 45 Minuten extensiv betrachtet. Die DVD-Szenen 5 – 8 (*A Different Perspective – Chances – Find your own Walk – Unorthodox Ideas*) beginnen mit Keatings *Lesson on Language* und enden damit, dass der stolze Knox ein Sandwich aus der Schulküche stiehlt.

Das lange Filmsegment wird en bloc präsentiert. Jede Schülerin/jeder Schüler hat ihr/sein spezielles Gruppen-Arbeitsblatt (vgl. Hausaufgabe 2.2 – *Worksheets* 7–11) vor sich, wodurch die Aufmerksamkeit auf bestimmte Aspekte gelenkt wird. Zusätzlich gibt es an alle die Aufforderung, kurze Stichpunkte zu den gestellten Aufgaben zu notieren. Als Hausaufgabe sind die Notizen auf den Arbeitsblättern zu ergänzen und zu reflektieren.

3.2 Jigsaw time

Nach dem *guided viewing* der Vorstunde erfolgt nun die Auswertung in Form eines sog. *Gruppenpuzzles*, einer speziellen Variante des Gruppenunterrichts.
Nachdem jede Schülerin/jeder Schüler ihr/sein Arbeitsblatt in der Vorstunde und zu Hause individuell bearbeitet hat, folgt die Expertenrunde. Diejenigen Schülerinnen/Schüler, die das gleiche Thema bearbeitet haben, treffen sich in ihrer Gruppe und unterstützen sich auf dem Weg zum Experten. Diese Phase dauert ca. 15 Minuten. Danach verlassen alle ihre Gruppen und bilden neue Fünfergruppen, in denen jeder Teilbereich durch einen Experten vertreten ist. In dieser ebenfalls 15-minütigen Phase unterrichtet jeder sein vorbereitetes Thema und beteiligt sich an der Diskussion. So findet in mehreren Gruppen parallel der gleiche Unterricht statt.
In einer letzten Phase – ebenfalls 15 Minuten – werden die Diskussionsergebnisse im Plenum integriert und ergänzt.

Hausaufgabe:

Based on your notes and the discussion today, prepare a three-minute expert speech, in which you outline the main results in your field.

Notizen:

Group 1
Keating & 5 Lessons

Task:

Try to answer the following five questions. While viewing the film, make short notes. At home reflect and elaborate on them.

1. *Lesson on Language*: What is language for?

2. *Point of View Lesson*: Why does Keating make the pupils jump on their desks?

3. *Soccer Lesson*: Write down one of the verses the boys recite while kicking the ball.

4. *Marching Lesson*: Why does Keating quote Frost's poem ("Two roads diverged in the wood, and I took the one less traveled by.")?

5. *Lesson for Charlie*: Does Keating approve of Charlie's behaviour in the chapel? Why (not)?

Group 2
Neil & Todd

Task:

Try to answer the following five questions. While viewing the film, make short notes. At home reflect and elaborate on them.

1. What does Neil shout to Todd and why?

2. What kind of letter does Neil write?

3. How does Todd behave in the *Yawp Lesson*?

4. What does the birthday present scene tell us about the relationship between Neil and Todd?

5. What does Mr Perry forbid Neil to do and how does Neil react?

Group 3
Charlie & Knox

Task:

Try to answer the following five questions. While viewing the film, make short notes. At home reflect and elaborate on them.

1. Compare Knox's mood on his way to the football stadium and back home.

2. What leitmotifs does Knox shout out when calling Chris?

3. What does Charlie announce in the 3rd cave meeting and why?

4. What letter has Charlie written and what does he do in Welton Academy Chapel?

5. Knox recites his poem in Chris' classroom. What does that mean for Knox's development?

Group 4
The badies: Mr Nolan & Mr Perry

Task:

Try to answer the following five questions. While viewing the film, make short notes. At home reflect and elaborate on them.

1. How does Nolan behave in Welton Academy Chapel?

2. How would you characterize Nolan when he punishes Charlie?

3. What does Nolan advise Keating to do and how does he try to achieve that?

4. What does Mr Perry tell his son?

5. What impression does Mr Perry make on Neil/the viewer?

Group 5
Cinematography & Atmosphere

Task:

Try to answer the following five questions. While viewing the film, make short notes. At home reflect and elaborate on them.

1. *Rock'n'roll-scene*: What is its function?

2. *Bagpipe-music-interlude*: What atmosphere is conveyed here and why?

3. *Ode-to-Joy-scene*: How do music, images, colours and camera movement contribute to the overall atmosphere here?

4. *Charlie's-punishment-scene*: What two close-ups emphasize Mr Nolan's sadistic attitude?

5. *Mr Perry-Neil-scene*: Comment on the close-ups.

Erwartungshorizont:

Group 1

1. "Language was invented to woo women."
2. to be able to look at things differently, to change one's perspective
3. "Oh, to struggle against great odds, to meet enemies undaunted!" – "To indeed be a god!"
4. to make pupils become individuals and do things their own way
5. No – "There is a time for daring, and there is a time for caution." (plus joke: "If it had been collect, it would have been daring", i.e. if Nolan would have had to pay)

Group 2

1. Carpe diem! – wants to take the initiative and become an actor
2. fakes a letter of permission ("... on behalf of my son N. P. ...")
3. reserved – inspired by Keating – emotional – coming out
4. Todd is unhappy about the same present as last year – Neil cheers him up – understanding and friendship
5. forbids him to take part in the play – Neil suffers

Group 3

1. first happy, then disappointed: Chris hugs Chat
2. Carpe diem = Knox encourages himself – Yawp = I did it
3. new name: Nuwanda – new identity, development
4. a letter in the school magazine pleading for girls to be admitted to Welton – fakes a telephone call: "It's God, Mr Nolan!"
5. seizes the day, has become courageous

Group 4

1. like a drill sergeant
2. brutal, sadistic
3. to quit his unorthodox teaching methods – addressing him "John", mentioning private details
4. forbids him to play Puck
5. authoritarian

Group 5

1. boys begin to seize the day
2. melancholic – *montage*: after the scene in which Neil fakes the letter – *foreshadowing* of problems
3. atmosphere: joy and happiness ⇒ closeness Keating and boys – music: Ode to Joy (Alle Menschen werden Brüder) – images: football, boys carrying Keating on their shoulders, sunset – colours: warm, beautiful – camera movement: fast, some slow motion
4. Nolan's hand closing the door – paddle
5. show the emotions of the two very intimately – antagonistic conflict becomes clear – viewers' identification heightened

Notizen:

____

____

Component 4:
Climax & Finale

4.1 Neil's suicide

Die neunte Szene der DVD (*Neil's Dream*) kann als Klimax des Films bezeichnet werden. Sie beginnt mit Neils Lüge gegenüber Keating, er hätte bereits mit seinem Vater über seine Pläne gesprochen. Danach findet die Aufführung von Shakespeares *Mittsommernachtstraum* in Henley Hall statt, wo Neil *standing ovations* für seine großartige Darstellung von Puck bekommt. Neil fährt mit seinem Vater heim und erschießt sich mit einem Revolver im väterlichen Büro. Die Szene endet, als Charlie Todd mit der Hiobsbotschaft aufweckt: „Neil is dead!"

Die 18 Minuten werden ohne Unterbrechung vorgeführt. Im Anschluss wird das Grobverständnis des Inhalts kurz überprüft:

What happened to Neil?

He killed himself with a gun in his father's office.

Why did he commit suicide?

He did not want to leave Welton, give up his acting plans and be enrolled in Braden Military School.

Die zweite Hälfte der Unterrichtsstunde konzentriert sich auf zwei in dieser Szene dominante Gestaltungsmittel: Symbolismus und Atmosphäre. Mit Hilfe eines Arbeitsblattes (*Worksheet 12*) sollen die Schülerinnen und Schüler im *Reißverschluss-Verfahren* (*Kugellager-Verfahren*) entsprechende Beispiele dieser beiden Termini untersuchen. Dazu setzen sich alle in zwei Vollkreisen gegenüber. Die Mitglieder des Innenkreises bewegen sich alle zwei Minuten im Uhrzeigersinn weiter, während die Mitglieder des Außenkreises sitzen bleiben. Dadurch erhält jede Schülerin/jeder Schüler im 2-Minuten-Intervall einen neuen Partner. Die auf dem Arbeitsblatt notierten Fragen werden jeweils in Partnerarbeit diskutiert. Beim zweiten Fragenkomplex (*atmosphere*) kann zur Abwechslung der Außenkreis zur Bewegung aufgefordert werden. Zum Ende der Stunde sollte ein kurzes integrierendes Plenumsgespräch stattfinden.

Erwartungshorizont:

1.1 symbol of virility, manhood, courage
1.2 contrast play – reality (angry father)
1.3 address to his father as well: apology for mistakes, wish for harmony
1.4 Neil's exit from life, i.e. suicide
1.5 Neil's extraordinary performance (cf. Keating: "Make your lives extraordinary")
1.6 Jesus' crown of thorns during crucifixion
1.7 careful positioning of slippers → Mr Perry's rigidity
1.8 Neil's life preconceived by his parents

2.1 Mr Perry: the judge – Neil: the accused
2.2 tension heightened
2.3 danger – Puck's final monologue ("If we shadows ...") – foreshadowing of death
2.4 mysterious and ominous silence
2.5 analogy to Jesus – stripped off one's essentials
2.6 extreme terror emphasized

Notizen:

Neil's Suicide – Symbolism and Atmosphere

1. Symbolism

Try to find out with your different partners what the following symbols may stand for:

1.1 a Red Indian warrior symbol on Charlie's chest

1.2 *A Midsummer Night's Dream* (a romantic fairy tale)

1.3 Puck's monologue: "If we shadows have offended … If you pardon, we will mend … Give me your hands …"

1.4 Neil's exit from the stage and from Henley Hall

1.5 The DPS boys shouting "Yawp!"

1.6 Puck's crown

1.7 the black slippers of Neil's father

1.8 Neil's pyjamas neatly laid out on his bed

2. Atmosphere

With your different partners, discuss what kind of atmosphere the following cinematographic devices create.

2.1 *Camera*: At the Perrys' house, the camera shows Mr Perry standing, hands in his pockets, and Neil sitting.

2.2 *Sound*: While Neil is putting on Puck's crown in his room, the music is getting louder and louder.

2.3 *Lighting*: The viewer only sees Neil's shadow on the wall.

2.4 *Sound*: When Neil is on his way to and then in his father's study, there is hardly any sound.

2.5 *Field size*: Neil's bare feet are shown in close-up.

2.6 *Camera speed*: Mr Perry's discovery of Neil's dead body is rendered in slow motion.

4.2 Oh Captain, my Captain!

Das 10. und letzte Segment der DVD beginnt mit der düsteren Winterlandschafts-Szene nach Neils Selbstmord und endet mit der dramatischen Respektbezeugung der Schüler für Keating. Dazwischen liegen die Verhöre der Jungen durch den Direktor.

Dieses emotional sehr bewegende Finale sollte man ohne wohlmeinende Zwischenkommentare auf die Schülerinnen und Schüler wirken lassen. Die ca. 17 Minuten werden deshalb en bloc präsentiert. Im Anschluss daran findet wieder ein ziemlich schülergesteuertes Rezeptionsgespräch statt.
In einem ersten Schritt erkundigt sich die Lehrperson nach dem allgemeinen Eindruck:

Can you describe your first impression of this finale?

Possible answers: moving, dramatic, happy vs. sad ending

Im zweiten Schritt können die Schülerinnen und Schüler offen gebliebene Punkte klären lassen:

Are there any things which are not clear to you?

Possible students' questions:
- What is Cameron's excuse for signing the paper? (honor code of school)
- Who signs the paper? (Cameron, Meeks, Pitts, Overstreet etc.)
- Who does not sign the paper? (Charlie Dalton)
- Does Todd Anderson sign the paper? (yes because of parents' pressure? no?)

Nach der Klärung von Verständnisproblemen werden schließlich in einem charakterzentrierten Bewertungsgespräch (How do you judge ... behaviour?) die folgenden Handlungsaspekte ergebnisoffen diskutiert:

How do you judge the boys' behaviour during Mr Nolan's interrogation?

Possible answers: betray Mr Keating – reasons for signing the paper understandable: fear of expulsion, pressure from headmaster/parents/peers – Cameron: coward traitor – Charlie: consistent with his previous behaviour

How do you judge Mr Nolan's behaviour?

Possible answers: authoritarian headmaster looking for a scapegoat – jealous of Mr Keating's appeal to students – consistent with previous behaviour – dogmatic, stubborn, ineffective English teacher – blaming Keating: correct decision

How do you judge Mr McAllister after the courtyard Latin lesson?

Possible answers: follows Keating's open air approach – understanding between him and Keating

How do you judge the boys' behaviour at the end?

Possible answers: courageous – Todd as the real hero – show respect and affection for their teacher – have learned Keating's lesson: integrity, independence?

How do you judge Keating's behaviour at the end?

Possible answers: has forgotten personal belongings – needs final act of support – wants to provoke Nolan – finally is proud of Todd Anderson

Component 5: After & Beyond

Der letzte Teil des Unterrichtsmodells, die *post-viewing phase*, soll in Form von Freiarbeit mit anschließender Präsentation stattfinden. Abhängig von Interesse und Zeit kann diese Phase zwischen 2 und 5 Stunden betragen.

5.1 Freiarbeit

Für die materialgeleitete Freiarbeit stehen zwölf Arbeitsblätter (Kopiervorlagen 1–12) zur Verfügung. Je nach Nutzungsintensität können diese zwischen ein und drei Stunden lang bearbeitet werden. Folgende Materialien werden an zwölf verschiedenen Orten im Klassenzimmer ausgelegt:

P

- Kopiervorlage: Talking Duel
- Kopiervorlage: Mock Trial
- Kopiervorlage: Open Questions
- Kopiervorlage: Who Is to Blame for Neil's Death?
- Kopiervorlage: Quotes
- Kopiervorlage: Theme 1: Realism vs Idealism
- Kopiervorlage: Theme 2: Conformity vs Freedom
- Kopiervorlage: Comparison Book – Film
- Kopiervorlage: Deleted Scenes
- Kopiervorlage: Audio Commentary
- Kopiervorlage: Trailer
- Kopiervorlage: Me, the Poet

Im Sinne von Freiarbeit sind die Schülerinnen und Schüler in den folgenden Bereichen frei:

- Wahl des Materials
- Wahl der Sozialform (Einzel-, Partner-, Gruppenarbeit)
- Wahl des Erarbeitungsmodus (mündlich, schriftlich – sofern keine Vorgaben)
- Bestimmung von Zeit/Dauer

Die Lehrperson hat sich in dieser Phase vornehmlich um folgende Aufgaben zu kümmern:

- Vorgaben für die Präsentationsphase (jede Schülerin/jeder Schüler muss sich später mindestens an einem Vortrag beteiligen)
- Beachtung der zweiten Komponente des Kompositums *Freiarbeit* durch die Schülerinnen und Schüler
- Einhaltung einer ruhig-konzentrierten Arbeitsatmosphäre
- Korrektur schriftlicher Arbeiten und Entwürfe
- Technische Logistik (PC, DVD-Player)
- Coach/Tutor/Mentor

5.2 Presentations

Nach der Phase der freien Arbeit werden die Ergebnisse im Klassenzimmer präsentiert. Je nach Interessenschwerpunkten der Schülerinnen/Schüler und Grad der Steuerung durch die Lehrperson kann dies eine oder zwei Stunden in Anspruch nehmen. Zumindest sollte auf der Vorgabe bestanden werden, dass jede Schülerin/jeder Schüler sich wenigstens einmal beteiligt. Denkbar ist auch eine Videoaufnahme der *presentations* oder eine Darbietung im Rahmen einer Schulveranstaltung.

Notizen:

Talking Duel

John Keating – charismatic pedagogue or irresponsible demagogue?

Pick a partner and fight a verbal duel. One of you argues that Mr Keating is a charismatic pedagogue. The other finds reasons why he behaves like an irresponsible demagogue.

Possible arguments pro Keating:

- unconventional teaching methods
- enthusiastic teacher
- talented in many fields (ex-captain of the football team, editor of the school annual, DPS member)
- emotional involvement with students' problems
- …

Possible arguments against Keating:

- not keeping to the curriculum
- unaware of possible consequences of his teaching principles
- giving Neil a wrong piece of advice
- egotistic/narcissistic tendencies
- …

Mock Trial

Mr John Keating has been charged with seducing young people, e.g. instigating Neil Perry to play Puck against Mr Perry's explicit will, thus causing Neil's suicide in the end.

To simulate a trial, the following parts must be prepared and played by pupils:

- the accused (John Keating)
- a judge
- a barrister (defence)
- a prosecutor
- two/three witnesses for the prosecution
- two/three witnesses for the defence
- a jury (six to twelve pupils)
- audience (rest of the class)

To simplify the trial, the following procedure is suggested:

1. The judge opens the trial, stating what Mr Keating is accused of.
2. The prosecutor explains why Mr Keating has been accused.
3. The barrister claims that the accused is innocent.
4. The witnesses for the prosecution and defence testify against/in favour of Keating.
5. The accused denies having committed a crime.
6. The prosecutor summarizes the charges and suggests a penalty.
7. The defence puts forward valid arguments for Keating and pleads "not guilty".
8. The jury retire and agree on a verdict.
9. The chairman of the jury pronounces the verdict.
10. The judge announces the penalty.

Instead of leaving the courtroom and chatting about the verdict, the members of the audience stay inside the classroom and are given the opportunity to comment on the trial.

Open Questions

Choose some of the following ten questions. Reflect on them individually or, preferably, discuss them with a partner or among a group.

1. Why did the original Dead Poets Society stop existing?
2. How did the poetry book get into Neil's room?
3. Did Todd sign the paper at the end?
4. Who was the bravest of Keating's boys?
5. Would Neil still have committed suicide if he had never met Mr Keating?
6. Was there any other answer than suicide for Neil?
7. Should teachers interfere in conflicts between students and parents?
8. Should teachers encourage nonconformism among their students?
9. Would you like to attend a school like Welton Academy?
10. *Open ending:* What does the future hold for Keating and the boys?

Who Is to Blame for Neil's Death?

Write down in a few sentences who is really to blame for Neil's death.

Is it …

a) Keating – for starting the ball rolling
b) Neil – for misunderstanding Keating's principles
c) Mr Perry – for being the prototype of an authoritarian father
d) Mrs Perry – for never contradicting her husband
e) Todd – for being too weak to keep Neil from playing Puck
f) Somebody else

Quotes

Sort the following quotes from the film into your private hit list. No. 1 is your favourite, No. 10 the one you like least.

a) A sport is a chance for us to have other human beings push us to excel.

b) To be a sailor of the world
Bound for all ports

c) To dance,
Clap hands,
Exalt,
Shout,
Skip,
Roll on,
Float on

d) To indeed be a god!

e) I sound my barbaric YAWP from the rooftops of the world.

f) I close my eyes, and this image floats beside me:
a sweaty-toothed madman with a stare that pounds my brain.
His hands reach out and choke me
and all the time he's mumbling, mumbling truth
like a blanket that always leaves your feet cold.

g) Laughing, crying, tumbling, mumbling,
gotta do more, gotta be more.
Chaos screaming, chaos dreaming,
gotta do more, gotta be more!

h) You gotta calm down. – No, that's just my problem. I've been calm all my life.

i) We all have a great need for acceptance,
but you must trust that your beliefs are unique, your own.
Some people may think them odd or unpopular.

j) Robert Frost said: Two paths diverged into the wood,
and I, I took the one less traveled by,
and that has made all the difference.

Theme 1: Realism vs Idealism

Welton is a traditional school for the elite. It is there to turn fine young boys into businessmen, doctors and other members of the established professions – not actors, poets or 'creative' people who lack materialistic ambitions. This makes it hard to believe that a teacher like John Keating is appointed there, and how he gets away with his teaching methods, especially in 1959.

The boys in Keating's class are open to new things. They are impressionable teenagers who are ready to take on anything new that is thrown their way. The conservative fifties seem to be coming to an end, and the rebellious generation is getting closer. This is already shown in Charlie and is shown more and more as you start to see the radical teaching methods.

Keating just seems to be in the wrong place at the wrong time. By inspiring the boys to "seize the day" and letting them dedicate themselves to airy and romantic notions of their own self realisation, he is really doing them wrong, but he doesn't see it.

Keating is shocked to hear about Charlie getting paddled for his prank in the assembly. It was almost as if he had no idea how much he had influenced the boys. Then when Neil kills himself he breaks down over his old poetry book. It seemed as though he was grieving for Neil, but also for his own lost youth at the same time. Also at no point is there any acceptance of responsibility or a realisation that he misjudged the situation of teaching the boys about self-realization. The trouble starts, and Keating stands down, unprepared to stand up for himself at all.

http://www10.pair.com/crazydv/weir/dps/

Questions:

1. In what forms are realism and idealism implied in this text?

2. How is Mr Keating judged here? Do you agree?

3. Which attitude towards life do you prefer – realism or idealism? Why?

Theme 2: Conformity vs Freedom

The four pillars of Welton Academy (Tradition, Excellence, Honour, Discipline) show the boys exactly what is expected of them: tradition. At Welton that means traditional teaching methods and teachers and a traditional curriculum. Keating challenges this tradition. He challenges it by encouraging the boys to think and act for themselves, to be their own and not conform if it is not what they want to do. He gives off the impression that taking risks and breaking the rules in the pursuit of one's pleasure is OK to do.

On a personal level, the theme of conformity is mainly focused at the relationship between Neil and his father. They couldn't be more different. All Neil wants to do is become an actor – to live out his dreams. He is intimidated by his strict and up-right father – a man who has stayed pulled together his whole life and has made sacrifices so that Neil could have the advantages he never had. He takes no nonsense, no disobedience and certainly has a negative opinion of Mr Keating and "this acting business". He will not ever give Neil the chance to express his own feelings about his own future. He may have struggled to get Neil to this expensive school so he wants to see value for his money. This is all he seems to see. He can't see Neil's pain and anger and ends up pushing him too far with a tragic consequence.

Afterwards the school closes ranks in a consolidated show of conformity, showing that those who fail to take on the "four pillars" at Welton stand no chance against it.

http://www10.pair.com/crazydv/weir/dps/

Questions:

1. How are conformity and freedom defined in this text?

2. How is Mr Perry judged here? Do you agree?

3. Which attitude towards life do you prefer – conformity or freedom? Why?

Comparison Book – Film

Chapter 14

The moon was full. The stars were out in abundance. The night was clear and cold. The trees hung heavy with icicles as the boys, Ginny, and Chris followed Mr Keating out into the night. The freeze had turned the barren forest into a world of sparkling diamonds. The group walked through the woods behind Keating as he recited: "The Saints smiled gravely and they said, 'He's come …'".
"Are you washed in the blood of the Lamb?" they chorused.
"Walking lepers followed rank on rank, lurching bravos from the ditches dank, drabs from the alleyways and drug fiends pale,/Minds still passion ridden, soul-powers frail …".
"Are you washed in the blood of the Lamb?" they repeated.

As the Society marched through the still of the night, an ominous silence settled over the Perry home. Mr and Mrs Perry got into bed and turned off their bedroom light. They did not hear the door to another room open. Neil walked into the hall. He turned a corner and slipped quietly downstairs.
Moonlight illuminated Mr Perry's study. Neil walked to his father's desk, opened the top drawer and reached way in the back. He pulled out a key and with it, he unlocked the bottom drawer of the desk. Neil sat in the leather desk chair and, reaching across the desk, he picked up the crown of flowers he'd worn as Puck and put it on his head.

The group stopped beside the waterfall, which had frozen. The icy sculpture seemed to defy the laws of gravity as the students looked at its remarkable form.The sky was incredibly clear. Moonlight bouncing off the snow cast a strange bluish glow on the group as Keating continued the poem:

"Christ came gently with a robe and crown, /For Booth the soldier, while the throng knelt down./ He saw King Jesus. They were face to face, /and he knelt a-weeping in that holy place."

"Are you washed in the blood of the Lamb?" they recited again.
The moonlight and the mystical wonder of the frozen waterfall combined with the magical poetry to set the group dancing and playing in the snow. They worked themselves into a joyful, frantic revelry.
Knox and Chris drifted away from the group and embraced. They kissed, soft and warm, under the frozen moon.

Mr and Mrs Perry were fast asleep when the quick, short sound broke the night's silence. "What was that?" Mr Perry sat up.
"What?" his wife asked, half-asleep.

"That sound? Didn't you hear it?"
"What sound?"
Mr Perry climbed out of bed and walked into the hallway. He walked up and down the hall, finally entering Neil's room. He ran out and down the stairs as Mrs Perry followed, trying to get her robe on over her flailing arms.
Mr Perry walked into the study and turned on the light. He looked around. Everything seemed normal, but just as he turned to leave, he spotted the glistening black object lying on the carpet – his revolver. Panicked, he moved around the desk until he saw the pale white hand. He gasped.
Neil lay on the floor, bathed in his own blood. Mr Perry knelt down and embraced his son while his wife let out an anguished scream.
"No!" Mr Perry cried. "No!"

Mr Keating and the boys took the girls home and returned to Welton in the early-morning hours.
"I'm wiped, drained," Todd said as he headed to his room. "I'm going to sleep until noon."
But early the next morning, Charlie, Knox, and Meeks walked into Todd's room. The boys' faces were ashen. They looked down at Todd, who snored peacefully.
"Todd, Todd," Charlie called softly.
Todd opened his eyes and sat up, looking exhausted. After a few moments, his eyes adjusted to the light. He closed them and lay back down. Then, feeling for his clock, he picked it up and squinted.
"It's only eight. I gotta sleep," he said, pulling the covers over his head. He sat up suddenly, his eyes wide open. His friends were still standing there, silent, and he sensed that something was wrong.
"Todd, Neil's dead. He shot himself," Charlie said.

[...]

N.H. Kleinbaum. *Dead Poets Society.* Hamburg: Petersen, 2002, pp. 148–151

Questions:

1. What differences between film and book can you recognize?

2. What parallels between the action in the Perrys' house and the poem recited by the group can you detect?

Deleted Scenes

One of the scenes which were deleted for the final version was a cave meeting after Neil's performance. Watch this scene (DVD Extras: Zusätzliche Szenen) and try to answer the following three questions:

1. Give a summary of the action in this scene.

2. Why does this scene run parallel to Neil's suicide in the Perrys' house? Consider the contents of the poem as well.

3. Why, do you think, did the director delete this scene from the final version?

Audio Commentary

One of the DVD Extras is an audio commentary. This means that the whole film is accompanied by comments from the director, cameraman and script writer.

Pick one scene from the film and listen to the audio commentary. You may listen several times to understand what the movie makers really say.

Questions:

1. Summarize how the director/cameraman/script writer comment on this scene.

2. Do you agree with their evaluation? Say why (not).

Trailer

Watch the movie trailer, which is part of the DVD Extras, and answer these three questions afterwards.

1. Do you think that this trailer is an appropriate summary of the movie?

2. What are typical features of trailers?

3. Is this trailer an appealing one, i.e. would it induce you to go to the movies?

Me, the Poet

All the poets quoted in *Dead Poets Society* are dead.
Why not be a living poet and “contribute a verse”?

You have got two options:

1. Individual poem

You can write your own poem on any topic you associate with the film *Dead Poets Society*. It may be a rather classical form with rhyme scheme and different stanzas. Or you may choose a modern form without rhyme, special metre or rhythm.

2. Class poem

You start a class poem by writing the first line on a piece of paper. Then you give it to a classmate who has to add a second line. The poem is complete when each pupil in the class has contributed a verse.

Lösungsvorschläge zu Kopiervorlagen 6, 7, 8, 9, 11

Kopiervorlage: Theme 1: Realism vs Idealism

1. a) realism: tradition, elite, preparing for established professions, materialistic ambitions, acceptance of responsibility
   b) idealism: creative people (actors, poets), unconventional teaching methods, seize the day, airy and romantic notions of self-realization
2. Keating is in the wrong place at the wrong time, misguides the students, misjudges the situation, ignores responsibility – pupils' judgements may vary

Kopiervorlage: Theme 2: Conformity vs Freedom

1. a) conformity: to stick to tradition/excellence/honor/discipline, Mr Perry's character, to close ranks against Keating
   b) freedom: to think and act for oneself, to be one's own, to take risks, to break rules in the pursuit of one's pleasure, to live out one's dreams
2. serious, strict, up-right, has stayed pulled together his whole life, has made sacrifices for his son, expects obedience, oppresses Neil, is blind to his son's problems, pushes him too far – pupils' judgements may vary

Kopiervorlage: Comparison Book – Film

1. the action which involves Keating and the group beside the waterfall is not shown in the film
2. poem: *General William Booth Enters into Heaven* by Vachel Lindsay
   - poem: reference to the death of Booth, the founder of the Salvation Army – Perrys' house: Neil's death
   - General Booth: military rank – Neil: threat of military school
   - chorus: Are you washed in the blood of the Lamb? – death of an innocent victim (lamb – Neil)
   - invoking Jesus Christ: crown of thorn – Puck's crown of flowers
   - author (Vachel Lindsay) also died by suicide
   - association with John Wilkes Booth: assassinated Abraham Lincoln, the "captain" of Whitman's *Oh Captain! My Captain!*

Kopiervorlage: Deleted Scenes

1. – Keating, the boys, Chris and Ginny walk through the winter forest to a frozen waterfall
   - Keating recites a poem (V. Lindsay's *General William Booth Enters into Heaven*), the group chorus "Are you washed in the blood of the Lamb?"
   - The group dance and play in the snow
   - They work themselves into a frantic revelry
   - Knox and Chris embrace and kiss
   - Keating and the boys take the girls home and return to Welton in the early hours of the morning
2. symbolic parallels and contrasts
   - parallels: frozen waterfall & Neil's death, cold night & Mr Perry's heartlessness
   - contrasts: joyful revelry vs utter despair, feeling of belonging vs isolation

3. – length: film lasts more than two hours, even without this scene
   – form: scene appears somewhat exaggerated, mannered, melodramatic

Kopiervorlage: Trailer

1. – yes: key scenes, main characters, hints at conflicts are presented
   – no: chronological order not maintained, ending not shown (cf. 2)
2. – form: summary of spectacular scenes in a mixed chronological order
   – function: to whet the viewers' appetite and induce them to go to the cinema, without revealing the ending
3. answers may vary

Notizen:

Internetadressen

http://www.mlenz.de/home.htm

http://www.suntimes.com/ebert/ebert_reviews/1989/06/357909.html

http://www.funet.fi/pub/culture/tv+film/reviews/D/DEAD_POETS_SOCIETY.0569

http://www10.pair.com/crazydv/weir/articles/articlec.html

http://www.geocities.com/CollegePark/5552/dps.htm

http://www.geocities.com/Hollywood/Academy/4734/

http://www.geocities.com/Paris/Cafe/4057/deadpoets.html

http://www.geocities.com/ResearchTriangle/3606/dps.html

http://www.deliriumsrealm.com/delirium/movies/dps.asp

http://www.vordingbg-gym.dk/km/deadpoet/

http://us.imdb.com/Title?0097165

http://www10.pair.com/crazydv/weir/dps/

Weiterführende Literatur

- Bosold, Bernhard. 1991. „Du lebst nur einmal. – Nutze den Tag.“ *Materialbrief RU* 3, Deutscher Katecheten-Verein, 1-5.
- Dirks, Una. 1994. „Mit Metaphern deuten lernen. Eine Unterrichtsreihe am Beispiel des Films ‚Dead Poets Society'. *Praxis des neusprachlichen Unterrichts* 2, 138-151.
- Fried, Hellmut. 1992. „Auf die Perspektive kommt es an! Der Film ‚Der Club der toten Dichter‘. *Praxis Schule 5-10*, 6, 52-53.
- Glatthorn, Allan. 1995. “Dead Poets: Live Issues.” *National Council of Teachers of English*. North Carolina.
- Grindhammer, Lucille. 1993. “Hollywood in the English Language Classroom: The Dead Poets Society”. *Neusprachliche Mitteilungen* 4, 244-250.
- Heilman, Robert. 1991. “The Great-Teacher Myth.” *American Scholar* 3, 417-423.
- Kleinbaum, Nancy. 1989. **Dead Poets' Society**. New York: Bantam.
- Hentzi, Gary. 1990. “Peter Weir and the Cinema of New Age Humanism.” *Film Quarterly* 2, 2-12.
- Krapf, Hans-Georg. 1997. **Nancy H. Kleinbaum. Dead Poets Society**. Münster: Aschendorff (*Aschendorffs Vokabularien*).
- Krüger-Kahloula, Angelika. 1992. “Recycling Dead Poets: An English Unit for the Upper Grades.” *Der Fremdsprachliche Unterricht* 8, 42-46.
- Liebelt, Wolf (Hg.). 1994. **Der Film Dead Poets Society im Englischunterricht**. (*Materialien zur Medienpädagogik der Landesmedienstelle Niedersachsen*)
- Meyer, Walter. 1994/95. „Dead Poets Society – Film und Buch im Englischunterricht der Klasse 10.“ *Materialien der Landesmedienstelle zu Film, Funk und Schulfernsehen Englisch* 2, 27-33.
- Novak, Ralph. 1989. “Dead Poets Society”. *PEOPLE* 23.
- Pickering, Samuel. 1991. “Speakeasy.” *Virginia Quarterly Review* 4, 722-745.
- Thal, Ortwin. 1990. „Frei sein für sich selbst. Der Club der toten Dichter.“ *Merz* 3, 164-168.

Unterrichtsmodelle und Textausgaben

EINFACH ENGLISCH

NEU

Edited by Hans Kröger

J. B. Priestley An Inspector Calls	by Hans Kröger Textausgabe. 80 S. kart., Best.-Nr. 041200 0 Unterrichtsmodell. 64 S., DIN A4, kart., Best.-Nr. 041201 0
T. C. Boyle The Tortilla Curtain	by Wiltrud Frenken, Angela Luz and Brigitte Prischtt Unterrichtsmodell. 75 S. DIN A4, kart., Best.-Nr. 041203 7
Charles Webb The Graduate	by Louise Nübold Unterrichtsmodell. 60 S. DIN A4, kart., Best.-Nr. 041205 3
Arthur Miller The Crucible	by Hans-Christoph Ramm Unterrichtsmodell. 84 S. DIN A4, kart., Best.-Nr. 041209 6
Monty Python	by Engelbert Thaler Unterrichtsmodell. 71 S. DIN A4, kart., Best.-Nr. 041221 5
William Golding Lord of the Flies	by Angela Luz, Brigitte Prischtt and Wiltrud Frenken Unterrichtsmodell. 98 S. DIN A4, kart., Best.-Nr. 041217 7
Mark Behr The Smell of Apples	by Anno Ortmeier Unterrichtsmodell. 77 S. DIN A4, kart., Best.-Nr. 041215 0
American Beauty	by Wiltrud Frenken, Brigitte Prischtt and Angela Luz Unterrichtsmodell. 87 S. DIN A4, kart., Best.-Nr. 041225 8
Criminals & Detectives	by Christine Hoidis-Fehler Textausgabe. 98 S., kart., Best.-Nr. 041206 1
Forrest Gump	by Kornelius Nelles and Karsten Witsch Unterrichtsmodell. 65 S. DIN A4, kart., Best.-Nr. 041231 2
Poetry	by Angela Luz Unterrichtsmodell. 103 S. DIN A4, kart., Best.-Nr. 041227 4

In Vorbereitung:

Criminals & Detectives	by Christine Hoidis-Fehler Unterrichtsmodell. ca. 85 S. DIN A4, kart., Best.-Nr. 041207 X
Thunderheart	by Wiltrud Frenken, Angela Luz und Brigitte Prischtt Unterrichtsmodell. ca. 80 S. DIN A4, kart., Best.-Nr. 041211 6
Roman Polanski: *Macbeth*	by Antje Blume Unterrichtsmodell. ca. 110 S. DIN A4, kart., Best.-Nr. 041235 5

Die Reihe wird fortgesetzt.

Fordern Sie unseren Prospekt zur Reihe an:
Informationen zum Nulltarif ✆ 08 00 / 1 81 87 87

SCHÖNINGH VERLAG
im Westermann Schulbuchverlag GmbH
Postfach 2540 · 33055 Paderborn

Schöningh

E-Mail: info@schoeningh.de
Internet: http://www.schoeningh.de